365 Days
in the
West Virginia
Penitentiary

C.J. Plogger

THANK YOU!

Fran Allred and Mickey Johnson of We Edit Books for your time, suggestions, and expertise. You made this project much better.

Donna Clark for formatting the pictures and arranging them to fit perfectly.

Janeen, my wife, who I want to spend every day of the rest of my life with.

JANUARY 1

He didn't want to go home

An inmate being released from the penitentiary told prison staff that he preferred to wait until spring and warmer weather.
Source: *Moundsville Weekly Echo*, Jan. 1, 1897

Taking his work home

Joe Ward, an assistant banker in Benwood, caused the bank to crash after taking $700,000. As a result, he ended up in the penitentiary.
Source: *Moundsville Daily Echo*, Jan. 1, 1932

Three dead in worst riot

The worst riot at the penitentiary started when the Avenger gang, led by Danny Lehman, took over the prison. The rioting prisoners seized some of the prison staff and murdered three inmates. The riot lasted until Jan. 3.
Source: *Wheeling News-Register*, Jan. 2, 1986

Gov. Arch Moore with a released hostage

JANUARY 2

Paul Burton executed in 1948

Paul Burton, a coal miner, received a death sentence for killing co-worker Willard Simpson. Burton had been fired from the mine because of serious altercations with Simpson and his brothers. Burton blamed them for his termination and, after a shift ended at the mine, waited for the brothers to come out of the portal. Running toward them from concealment, he fired at them. One of the shots struck Willard Simpson in the back. Burton was hanged and pronounced dead 11 minutes after he plummeted through the trap door.

Source: *"Pronounced Dead"* by C.J. Plogger

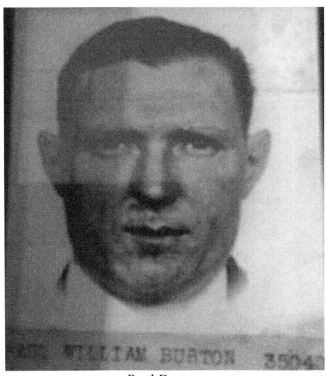

Paul Burton

JANUARY 3

William Gordon executed in 1947

William Gordon was executed for shooting Josephine Carr in the back while she was sitting at a sewing machine. According to accounts of the killing, Gordon simply snapped before pulling the trigger. At the time of the murder, Gordon was staying with the Carr family after telling its members that he had served in the Navy with their son during World War II. No one from Gordon's family claimed his body and it remained in a local funeral home for an extended time. He was hanged and pronounced dead.

Source: *"Pronounced Dead"* by C.J. Plogger

William Gordon

JANUARY 4

First triple hanging in 1924

Black Hand gang members, Dick Ferri, Nick Salamante, and Philip Connizzaro were executed for the murder of 26-year-old Frank Napolitano. The Black Hand gang formed in 1750 and emigrated from Italy to the U.S. in 1900. The gang composed letters to families threatening kidnapping, arson, or murder and signed them with a handprint that had been dipped in black ink. They were hanged together and at approximately 5:10 p.m. they were pronounced dead.
Source: *"Pronounced Dead"* by C.J. Plogger

Dick Ferri

Philip Connizzaro

Nick Salamante

JANUARY 5

A day off work and a movie

Inmates received a work holiday because of New Year's and were treated to a moving picture show presented by the Orpheum Theater.
Source: *Moundsville Weekly Echo*, Jan. 5, 1912

Penitentiary theater

Prison factories provided jobs

Four hundred-seventeen inmates worked at the Kleeson and Birdall factories in the penitentiary.
Source: *Moundsville Daily Echo*, Jan. 5, 1937

JANUARY 6

Not in the holiday spirit

Inmates Joe Wade and David Elliot lighted a Christmas tree on fire in the prison hallway. There was no major damage.
Source: *Moundsville Daily Echo*, Jan. 6, 1983

Last murder at the penitentiary

In 1995, inmate Robert Quimby became the last prisoner murdered at the penitentiary. The prison was in the process of closing and all inmates were being moved to other facilities. Most were transferred to the Mount Olive Correctional Complex in Montgomery.
Source: *West Virginia Penitentiary Death Book*

Mount Olive Correctional Complex

JANUARY 7

Greely Blankenship executed in 1935

Greely Blankenship never forgot his first love. While living in Kentucky, he returned to West Virginia to convince his first sweetheart to live with him, his wife, and their two children in the Bluegrass State. The sweetheart was married and her husband did not want her to go so he followed the woman and Blankenship. When the husband would not stop his pursuit, Blankenship shot him three times, killing him instantly. Blankenship was hanged and pronounced dead at 12:16 p.m.
Source: *"Pronounced Dead"* by C.J. Plogger

Greely Blankenship

JANUARY 8

Maybe it was homemade perfume

Inmate Mike Koski's 12-year-old son, Alex, came to visit him in the penitentiary and he gave the boy a small bottle filled with a muddy-ish yellow liquid to pour into his mother's coffee. It was presumed to be poison, but was thrown away so no determination of what it was could be made.
Source: *Moundsville Weekly Echo*, Jan. 8, 1909

Expensive building

A new building to house female inmates was proposed at an estimated cost of $243,000. Two years later, with no progress on construction, the female inmates were moved from the penitentiary.
Source: *Moundsville Daily Echo*, Jan. 8, 1945

Original building for female inmates

JANUARY 9

Up and over

Inmates Bordon and Moore escaped over the wall of the penitentiary by scaling a ladder.
Source: *Moundsville Weekly Echo*, Jan. 9, 1919

Dangerous work

Methane gas was extremely dangerous for the inmates working in the penitentiary mine located outside the walls of the penitentiary.
Source: *Moundsville Daily Echo*, Jan. 9, 1943

Prison coal mine

JANUARY 10

Not a fashion statement

Inmates who had previously escaped were required to wear striped prison clothing that indicated to correctional officers the need to watch them more closely.
Source: *Moundsville Daily Echo*, Jan. 10, 1931

Earl Dudding in stripes and author of *"Trail of the Dead Years"*

Interesting name, old chap

The chaplain for the penitentiary in 1967 was Ernest Sinfield. He was born in England.
Source: *Moundsville Daily Echo*, Jan. 10, 1967

JANUARY 11

Religious guidance

West Virginia Gov. George W. Atkinson signed a law requiring a chaplain at the penitentiary.

Source: *Moundsville Weekly Echo*, Jan. 11, 1901

Beasts of burden downsized

Mechanized equipment to haul coal out of the prison mine to the penitentiary replaced the mules that had been doing the job.
Source: *Moundsville Daily Echo*, Jan. 11, 1951

Inside the prison coal mine

JANUARY 12

Protective of her property

Mrs. William Brown, who confessed she had shot a young boy because he repeatedly took blackberries from her property, was convicted of second-degree murder and incarcerated at the penitentiary.
Source: *Moundsville Weekly Echo*, Jan. 12, 1906

Helping inmates

Warden Orel Skeen started an educational program for high school and college credits to be earned by the inmates.
Source: *Moundsville Daily Echo*, Jan. 12, 1948

Education wing in new administration building

JANUARY 13

High fare

Escaped inmates George Vacovich and Oley Holsclaw kidnapped taxi driver Lloyd Stern and forced him to drive them to Pennsylvania.
Source: *Moundsville Daily Echo*, Jan. 13, 1960

Expensive windows

Acting Warden Arthur L. McKenzie asked the state of West Virginia for $45,000 to replace the windows the inmates had broken out on New Year's Eve.
Source: *Moundsville Daily Echo*, Jan. 13, 1976

Broken window in non-contact visitation room

JANUARY 14

Escapees go on robbery spree

After inmates William Spencer and Elwood McClure escaped from the penitentiary, they traveled throughout Ohio robbing banks.
Source: *Moundsville Daily Echo*, Jan. 14, 1944

Money for new cells

In 1949, the penitentiary received $1,164,180 to build new cells in the south part of the building.
Source: *Moundsville Daily Echo*, Jan. 14, 1949

J Block of new wall

JANUARY 15

Not thirsty

During the construction of a new wall of the penitentiary, inmate William Lungh was sent for a bucket of water and never returned.
Source: *Moundsville Daily Echo*, Jan. 15, 1935

Prison farm

Warden Orel Skeen named the prison farm "Camp Fair Chance." Because of the many escapes, the inmates called it "Camp Sure Chance."
Source: *Moundsville Daily Echo*, Jan. 15, 1954

Prison farm

JANUARY 16

Promoted to the Big House

Warden O.C. Boles was the sheriff of Wood County before he was appointed warden of the penitentiary. Source: *Moundsville Daily Echo*, Jan. 16, 1960

Warden O.C. Boles

JANUARY 17

New way of walking

In a major step in prison reform, inmates were no longer required to walk in "lockstep." The practice was used when inmates were marched in a military drill style and had to hold the waist of the person in front of them.
Source: *Moundsville Weekly Echo*, Jan. 17, 1896

"Lockstep"

Conviction overturned by racial prejudice claim

Matilene Dean murdered Mack Nixon in self-defense and was sentenced to be hanged at the penitentiary, but her conviction was overturned because of racial prejudice.
Source: *Moundsville Daily Echo*, Jan. 17, 1950

Mad!

The inmates were angry because they were no longer allowed to wear blue jeans, which were replaced by prison khaki clothes.
Source: *Moundsville Daily Echo*, Jan. 17, 1990

JANUARY 18

Inmate legally represented himself in court

Charles Coon was the first inmate at the penitentiary to legally represent himself in a court of law. His trial started on this date.
Source: *Moundsville Weekly Echo*, Jan. 18, 1918

Short vacation

Fifty-four inmates were able to stay out of their cells for two hours after they threatened a correctional officer with an icepick and took his keys.
Source: *Moundsville Daily Echo*, Jan. 18, 1968

West Virginia Penitentiary keys

JANUARY 19

Penitentiary captain assaults newspaper editor

Capt. Reece was not a pleasant man and was rough with inmates. He was unhappy when some of his altercations were reported in the local newspaper and went to the news office and assaulted editor Sam Shaw by pushing him down three times.

Source: *Moundsville Weekly Echo*, Jan. 19, 1900

Moundsville Echo Editor Sam Shaw

JANUARY 20

Not obeying the law

Leo Belinkski was sent to the penitentiary for having and operating a whiskey still.
Source: *Moundsville Weekly Echo*, Jan. 20, 1922

Moonshine still

JANUARY 21

Prison mine operating

The prison mine became operational. Its depth was 80 feet, six inches.
Source: *Moundsville Weekly Echo*, Jan. 21, 1921

Inmate wanted out of protective custody

Inmate Randy Thomas was placed in protective custody, but wanted to go back to the general population. The prison staff was against the move and denied it, so Thomas sued the penitentiary.
Source: *Moundsville Daily Echo*, Jan. 21, 1988

Cell in protective custody

JANUARY 22

A lot of sickness

One hundred of the 600 inmates were severely ill with cases of influenza.
Source: *Moundsville Weekly Echo*, Jan. 22, 1897

Presidential denial

Inmate Houston Whiting was sentenced to the penitentiary for 18 years, but pursued a pardon from President Grover Cleveland. Cleveland denied his pardon and he had to serve out his sentence.
Source: *Moundsville Weekly Echo*, Jan. 22, 1897

President Grover Cleveland

JANUARY 23

Psychological tests required for new officers

A legislative bill was passed in 1980 that required correctional officers to complete psychological testing before starting work in a prison.
Source: *Moundsville Daily Echo*, Jan. 23, 1980

West Virginia Penitentiary correctional officers

JANUARY 24

Not very appreciative

Andrew Maura was associated with the Black Hand gang and spent a year at the penitentiary. His loving wife diligently worked to have him released early and she was successful. He displayed his appreciation by stabbing her in the chest once then stabbing himself twice. Both recovered.
Source: *Moundsville Weekly Echo*, Jan. 24, 1902

Violating interstate rules

The Kleeson factory, which operated within the walls of the penitentiary, was found guilty of violating the Hawes-Cooper Act. This act regulated interstate shipments of prison manufactured goods.
Source: *Moundsville Daily Echo*, Jan. 24, 1939

Factory in prison

JANUARY 25

Almost the first electrocution

Cecil Harless almost became the first man to be executed by "Old Sparky" because he criminally assaulted his 11-year-old daughter.
Source: *Moundsville Daily Echo*, Jan. 25, 1950

"Old Sparky"

JANUARY 26

Low pay

In 1984, the *Moundsville Daily Echo* reported that the pay for correctional officers was "reaching a point of desperation."
Source: *Moundsville Daily Echo*, Jan. 26, 1984

Moundsville Echo building

JANUARY 27

Blizzard

A blizzard blowing through the area slowed down two correctional officers from arriving at the penitentiary with four inmates.
Source: *Moundsville Weekly Echo*, Jan. 27, 1905

Winter storm coming into Moundsville

JANUARY 28

Scissor assault

Inmate John Smokey picked up a pair of scissors after he was confronted by Correctional Officer J.M. Williams for trying to leave the building through the wrong door. Smokey jumped on Williams and sliced his left ear. The wound was not serious and Williams was able to stay on duty.

Source: *Moundsville Weekly Echo*, Jan. 28, 1921

A weapon made by inmates

JANUARY 29

Robert Ford executed in 1926

Robert Ford was a burly man and the tallest to be hanged. Ford's death sentence resulted from Ed Woody confronting Ford because Woody thought Ford was flirting with his wife. They began to fist fight, but Ford pulled out a revolver and fatally shot Woody. Ford was hanged and pronounced dead at 5:22 p.m.
Source: *"Pronounced Dead"* by C.J. Plogger

Robert Ford

JANUARY 30

Mark McCauley executed in 1948

Mark McCauley was about to be arrested by three law enforcement officials for stealing a truck. As they approached his house, he fired at them with a shotgun killing two of them, West Virginia State Trooper Joseph Horne and Tucker County Sheriff O.G. Hovatter. McCauley was hanged and pronounced dead at 9:12 p.m. Source: *"Pronounced Dead"* by C.J. Plogger

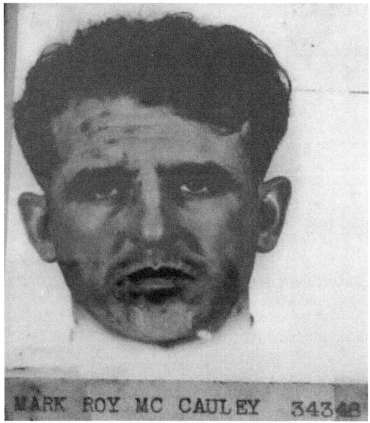

Mark McCauley

JANUARY 31

Cow stealing

Two men were brought to the penitentiary from Wetzel
County to serve a two-year sentence for stealing cows.
Source: *Moundsville Weekly Echo*, Jan. 31, 1908

Cattle at prison farm

Tuberculosis deaths

In 1937, 13 inmates died from tuberculosis.
Source: *Moundsville Daily Echo*, Jan. 31, 1938

FEBRUARY 1

Administrator named

Robert Wells became chief clerk at the penitentiary.
Source: *Moundsville Daily Echo*, Feb. 1, 1943

Entrance into older administration building

FEBRUARY 2

An unruly officer

Correctional Officer Dunn was drunk when he ran into Harry Johnston and they exchanged heated words at a bar. Johnston grabbed Dunn's billy club and beat him over the head with it.
Source: *Moundsville Weekly Echo*, Feb. 2, 1900

Ready to use

"Old Sparky," the electric chair that was built by inmate Paul Glenn, was ready for use on this day in 1950.
Source: *Moundsville Daily Echo,* Feb. 2, 1950

Buttons pushed to activate "Old Sparky"

FEBRUARY 3

Wesley Swain executed in 1928

Wesley Swain sexually assaulted five-year-old Aurelia Thompson but never admitted to the sadistic crime, blaming his behavior upon the overuse of liquor. His last words when they placed the black hood over his head were, "Don't pull it down too far." He was hanged and pronounced dead at 9:07 p.m.
Source: *"Pronounced Dead"* by C.J. Plogger

Wesley Swain

FEBRUARY 4

Investigators seek evidence of cruelty

A legislative investigating committee was appointed by Gov. William M.O. Dawson to investigate claims of cruelty at the penitentiary.
Source: *Moundsville Weekly Echo*, Feb. 4, 1907

A lot of animals

At the prison farm, there were 400 hogs, 2,000 chickens, and 73 cows.
Source: *Moundsville Daily Echo*, Feb. 4, 1965

Chicken house at the prison farm

FEBRUARY 5

Smallpox in the penitentiary

Two inmates were diagnosed with smallpox and were moved to the prison farm so that they could not infect other inmates.
Source: *Moundsville Weekly Echo*, Feb. 5, 1909

Fire damage

A fire in the penitentiary caused $19,000 of damage.
Source: *Moundsville Weekly Echo*, Feb. 25, 1926

1926 fire in the penitentiary

FEBRUARY 6

Got wet

A little boy walking along the edge of the prison fountain slipped and fell in. His cries were heard by a correctional officer who ran out and rescued him.
Source: *Moundsville Weekly Echo*, Feb. 6, 1914

Prison fountain

Striking inmates want better food

Inmates went on strike for five days in 1972 because they were upset about the quality of the food.
Source: *Moundsville Daily Echo*, Feb. 6, 1972

FEBRUARY 7

Innovative way to escape

Seven inmates were caught trying to blow up North Hall so they could escape.
Source: *Moundsville Daily Echo*, Feb. 7, 1969

World-traveling adviser

Warden Donald Bordenkircher took an 11-week leave of absence from the penitentiary to travel to Saudi Arabia to advise that nation on how to improve its prisons.
Source: *Moundsville Daily Echo*, Feb. 7, 1975

Warden Donald Bordenkircher

FEBRUARY 8

Henry Grogan executed in 1929

Henry Grogan was convicted of the indecent assault of 27-year-old Mary Delle Akers, but he firmly claimed he only struck her after she tried to hit him with a stick. Mary never got over the assault and shot herself in the head, which led to her death. Grogan called his relatives before he was executed. This was the first time a condemned inmate talked to family on the phone. He was hanged and pronounced dead at 9:11 p.m.
Source: *"Pronounced Dead"* by C.J. Plogger

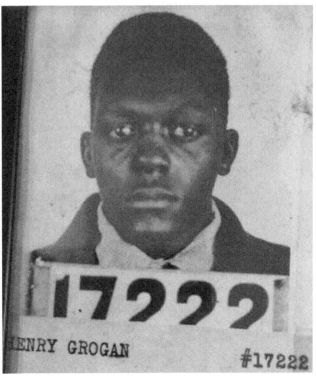

Henry Grogan

FEBRUARY 9

'Yap from Kanawha'

An inmate escaped and was later apprehended in the woods and returned to the penitentiary. A prison official was enraged that the newspaper printed an article about the escape so the *Moundsville Weekly Echo* labeled him "Yap from Kanawha."
Source: *Moundsville Weekly Echo*, Feb. 9, 1900

Moundsville Echo office

Suicide

Inmate Joseph Taylor committed suicide in his cell because he was distraught about spending the rest of his life in prison.
Source: *Moundsville Weekly Echo*, Feb. 9, 1906

FEBRUARY 10

Dangerous facility

Warden M.E. Ketchum stated that the penitentiary was a "fire trap" because of the antiquated condition of the older cells. Ketchum's son, Philip Ketchum, was a correctional officer who was killed in the line of duty in 1941.
Source: *Moundsville Daily Echo*, Feb. 10, 1945

Warden M.E. Ketchum

FEBRUARY 11

New cell

Pierce Jeffries, 20, is moved to the death cells to await his execution for the murder of Mrs. William Vance. Source: *"Pronounced Dead"* by C.J. Plogger

Pierce Jeffries

FEBRUARY 12

Female workers at the penitentiary

The Gordon Shirt Co. was built in the penitentiary; it employed only female inmates.
Source: *Moundsville Weekly Echo*, Feb. 12, 1926

Women working in a shirt factory

FEBRUARY 13

Dangerous work

An inmate lost a finger and another lost an eye working in the factories in the penitentiary.
Source: *Moundsville Weekly Echo*, Feb. 13, 1903

Politicians caught accepting bribes

Sen. Ben Smith and four delegates, S. Rhodes, Rath Duff, David Hill, and H. Ashbury, were sent to the penitentiary for five- to 10-year sentences for receiving bribes in connection with a senatorial election.
Source: *Moundsville Weekly Echo*, Feb. 13, 1914

Gov. William Barron, first West Virginia chief executive convicted of a federal crime

Not a high salary

In 1947, the salary for the warden of the penitentiary was $5,000 a year.
Source: *Moundsville Daily Echo*, Feb. 13, 1947

FEBRUARY 14

Taboo charge

In 1896, Jack Pennington of Mercer County was brought to the penitentiary to serve two years for an incest conviction.
Source: *Moundsville Weekly Echo*, Feb. 14, 1896

Too much love

John Downey was sentenced to the penitentiary for bigamy.
Source: *Moundsville Daily Echo*, Feb. 14, 1946

Which wife of Downey visited him?

FEBRUARY 15

Sam Muratore executed in 1924

Sam Muratore, a member of the Black Hand gang, murdered James Shapira because he refused to give money to the gang. Muratore had been scheduled to be executed in the first triple hanging, which consisted of other Black Hand members, on Jan. 4, 1924, but received a reprieve. He was hanged and pronounced dead at 5:28 p.m.

Source: *"Pronounced Dead"* by C.J. Plogger

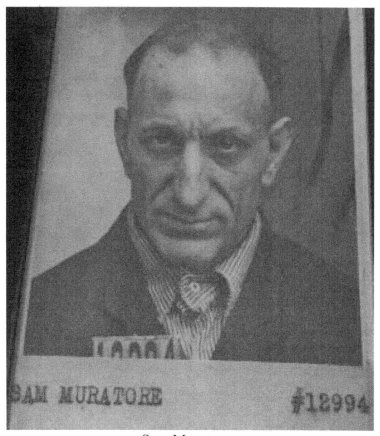

Sam Muratore

FEBRUARY 16

Didn't want to pay for stamps

George Beavers and a senator from New York were convicted of bribery and conspiracy to defraud the government on postal supplies. Beavers was sentenced to spend two years in the Moundsville penitentiary. Source: *Moundsville Weekly Echo*, Feb. 16, 1906

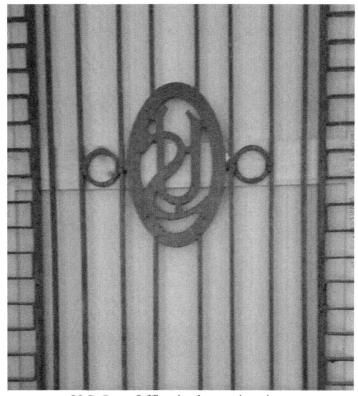

U.S. Post Office in the penitentiary

FEBRUARY 17

Frank Stevenson executed in 1911

Frank Stevenson thought Boles Blagman was having an affair with his wife, so he killed him with a handgun. Stevenson convinced authorities he was insane and was sent to the State Hospital in Weston. But the superintendent watched Stevenson carefully and determined he was sane because he was plotting to escape. Stevenson was not hanged until four years after his crime.

Source: *"Pronounced Dead"* by C.J. Plogger

Frank Stevenson

FEBRUARY 18

Pierce Jeffries executed in 1927

Pierce Jeffries viciously sexually assaulted Mrs. William Vance and was sentenced to death. Jeffries was hanged and pronounced dead at 5 p.m.
Source: *"Pronounced Dead"* by C.J. Plogger

Pierce Jeffries

FEBRUARY 19

Many spectators

Five hundred people came to the penitentiary to watch a boxing match.
Source: *Moundsville Daily Echo*, Feb. 19, 1935

Innovative escape

On Feb. 19, Tomie Mollohan, David Williams, and Fred Hamilton escaped by burrowing a tunnel from the greenhouse underneath the wall near Tower No. 3.
Source: *Wheeling Intelligencer*, Feb. 19, 1992

Tomie Mollohan

FEBRUARY 20

Double hanging

Emory Stephens and Will Adams were executed together in 1931. Stephens was sentenced to death after an intense argument with taxi driver Leonard Ooten resulted in Stephens beating him to death. At Stephen's execution, Ooten's father, Henry, was among the 32 witnesses.
Source: *"Pronounced Dead"* by C.J. Plogger

Emory Stephens

Will Adams snapped and murdered his ex-wife, Flossie Adams, and her aunt, Cynthia Maguire, while they were walking along the railroad tracks. He then went to the home of his former mother-in-law, Mallie Campbell, and sadistically killed her. Stephens and Adams were hanged and pronounced dead at 9:11 p.m.
Source: *"Pronounced Dead"* by C.J. Plogger

Will Adams

FEBRUARY 21

Stranded by floodwaters

Two groups of inmates from southern West Virginia could not be transported to the penitentiary because the trains could not travel through high waters.
Source: *Moundsville Weekly Echo*, Feb. 21, 1908

Training costs high

In 1976, the educational and vocational programs at the penitentiary cost $184,702 to run.
Source: *Moundsville Daily Echo*, Feb. 21, 1976

Door to educational classroom

FEBRUARY 22

More bacon needed

The penitentiary was at its highest population ever with 482 inmates. Twenty-three large hogs had to be butchered each day in order to feed them.
Source: *Moundsville Weekly Echo*, Feb. 22, 1895

Inmates in North Yard

FEBRUARY 23

Lawsuit

Inmate Michael Skinner sued the penitentiary for $10,000 because he had four fingers crushed while operating the license stamping machine.
Source: *Moundsville Daily Echo*, Feb. 23, 1977

Inmates working in a penitentiary factory

FEBRUARY 24

Construction started on Death House

Construction on the Death House and gallows was started to comply with a legislative act passed by the governor that all executions would take place inside the walls of the West Virginia Penitentiary.
Source: *Moundsville Weekly Echo*, Feb. 24, 1899

West Virginia Penitentiary Death House

FEBRUARY 25

Bud Peterson executed in 1949

Bud Peterson murdered Bessie Wright because she would not give him money to play poker. He was the last inmate hanged and subsequent executions occurred on "Old Sparky," the prison's electric chair. Peterson was hanged and pronounced dead at 9:11 p.m.

Source: *"Pronounced Dead"* by C.J. Plogger

Bud Peterson

FEBRUARY 26

No more federal prisoners

U.S. Attorney General Charles J. Bonaparte decided that no more federal prisoners would be sent to the penitentiary in Moundsville. Federal prisoners with two or fewer years to serve were sent to the Atlanta Federal Penitentiary and those with more than two years to serve were sent to Fort Leavenworth Federal Penitentiary.
Source: *Moundsville Weekly Echo*, Feb. 26, 1909

U.S. Attorney General Charles J. Bonaparte

FEBRUARY 27

Joint investigation

A joint committee of the West Virginia Senate and House sent a team to Moundsville to investigate charges of mismanagement and complaints of horrible conditions at the penitentiary.
Source: *Moundsville Weekly Echo*, Feb. 27, 1925

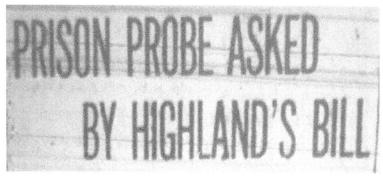

Moundsville Weekly Echo headline

FEBRUARY 28

Three strikes and you're out

James Graham was convicted of three different crimes under three different names and finally the court sentenced him to life in prison because of his failure to stop committing crimes.
Source: *Moundsville Weekly Echo*, Feb. 28, 1908

Another James Graham buried in White Gate Cemetery

MARCH 1

Distinct sounds of sirens

The penitentiary siren had two signals that indicated different events. A steady, long blast reported an escape, and short, quick blasts were an alert that there had been an escape from the prison farm, Camp Fair Chance. Source: *Moundsville Daily Echo*, March 1, 1955

Siren in South Yard

MARCH 2

George Carter executed in 1902

George Carter and Virgie Whistler were gambling with dice and started furiously arguing. Carter pulled a pistol from his pocket and killed Whistler, but later argued the shooting was in self-defense. Carter was hanged and pronounced dead at 6:56 p.m.

Source: *"Pronounced Dead"* by C.J. Plogger

George Carter

MARCH 3

Leroy Williams executed in 1922

Leroy Williams sexually assaulted Maud Stephens and then placed her face on a hot grate in front of a blazing fireplace. Her face was scarred and disfigured for the rest of her life. Williams was hanged and no one claimed his body, so it was sent to West Virginia University to be dissected by medical students.
Source: *"Pronounced Dead"* by C.J. Plogger

Leroy Williams

MARCH 4

Parolee commits foolish crime

Paroled inmate Bruce Von Leer held two teenagers captive for 14 hours in Wheeling.
Source: *Moundsville Daily Echo*, March 4,1961

Wheeling, West Virginia

MARCH 5

Ill warden

Warden J.Z. Terrell was stricken with severe rheumatism and taken to a hospital in Mount Clemens, Michigan.
Source: *Moundsville Echo*, March 5, 1920

JOSEPH Z. TERRELL
Warden J.Z. Terrell

Sleeping in the band room

The penitentiary was extremely overcrowded with 1,850 inmates, so some were forced to sleep in the band room.
Source: *Moundsville Weekly Echo*, March 5, 1926

MARCH 6

Henry Green executed in 1914

Henry Green and Mary Belle Justice lived together as an unmarried couple. One day the obsessively jealous Green returned from work and found three men in their house. Blinded by rage, Green shot and killed her. He was hanged and pronounced dead at 5:10 p.m.
Source: *"Pronounced Dead"* by C.J. Plogger

Henry Green

MARCH 7

Dangerously overcrowded

In 1931, there were 2,502 inmates in the penitentiary.
Source: *Moundsville Daily Echo*, March 7, 1931

Inmates spending time in North Yard

MARCH 8

Unusual duty

Warden M. Van Pelt and Correctional Officer Wickline took three inmates to court in Hinton to give evidence in a felony case. The duties of the warden were diverse. Source: *Moundsville Weekly Echo*, March 8, 1895

Courthouse in Hinton, West Virginia

MARCH 9

Scared straight

In 1970, juvenile probationers were taken to the penitentiary once a month to try to discourage them from continuing their wayward behavior.
Source: *Moundsville Daily Echo*, March 9, 1970

Still photo from original *"Scared Straight"* movie in 1978

MARCH 10

Jesse Cook executed in 1911

Jesse Cook once saved Frank Bennett's life, but later Cook thought Bennett was acting improperly toward his wife on Christmas Day. A discussion between the men quickly turned into an angry melee and Cook fatally stabbed his former best friend. Cook's wife, Mary, wrote to the governor and said if her husband were hanged that she would commit suicide. No records can be found to determine if she carried out her threat.

Source: *"Pronounced Dead"* by C.J. Plogger

JESSE COOK   #7499

Jesse Cook

MARCH 11

First Correctional Officer killed

Correctional Officer Earl Langfitt was the first officer to die at the penitentiary on this date in 1926. Inmate Henry Jackson stabbed him in the neck in the dining hall and Langfitt did not survive.
Source: *"Pronounced Dead"* by C.J. Plogger

Correctional Officer Earl Langfitt

MARCH 12

Terrible sentence

Milton McCracken was extremely intoxicated when he shot his 21-month-old son, Gene, on Christmas Eve because the baby was making too much noise. McCracken was convicted of second-degree murder, but, because he was drunk, he served just eight years for the crime.

Source: *Moundsville Weekly Echo*, March 12, 1909

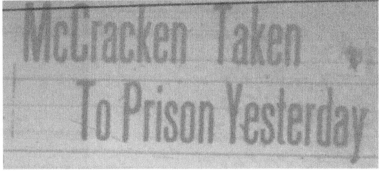

Moundsville Weekly Echo headline

MARCH 13

1930 fire

A fire started in the Bunk House of the penitentiary from a discarded cigarette.
Source: *Moundsville Daily Echo*, March 13, 1930

License plates

The inmates start making license plates on this day in 1933.
Source: *Moundsville Daily Echo*, March 13, 1933

MARCH 14

Chaplain's duties

Chaplain D.W. Ruble began work and was placed in charge of the library. He also handled all mail that came into the penitentiary. His salary was $900 a month.
Source: *Moundsville Weekly Echo*, March 14, 1902

Inside current West Virginia Penitentiary Chapel

MARCH 15

Evangelist Billy Sunday visited the penitentiary

Traveling evangelist Billy Sunday spoke at the prison and every shop was closed so that all inmates could attend. The former professional baseball player preached for an hour.

Source: *Moundsville Weekly Echo*, March 15, 1912

Evangelist Billy Sunday

MARCH 16

New prison act did not pass

In 1971, the West Virginia Legislature proposed building another maximum-security prison in Moundsville for $2,000,000 but the proposal did not pass.
Source: *Moundsville Daily Echo*, March 16, 1971

Mad barber

Moundsville barber, Denzil Butler was unhappy with the penitentiary because inmates were cutting hair for $1 and he charged $6.
Source: *Moundsville Daily Echo*, March 16, 1991

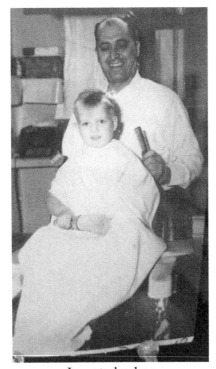

Inmate barber

MARCH 17

William Furbish executed in 1911

William Furbish sexually assaulted Flora Anglin on Christmas Eve. Furbish arranged to have prison chaplain, Dr. Riker, read his confession after he was hanged. The confession said that he committed the crime and he "was in liquor or I would not have done it."
Source: *"Pronounced Dead"* by C.J. Plogger

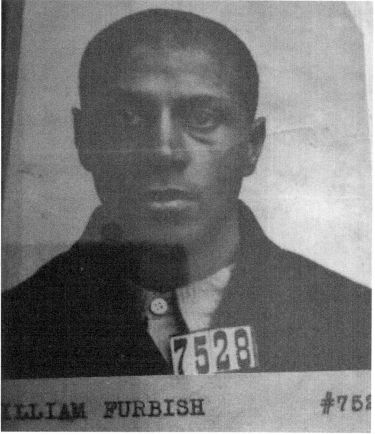

William Furbish

MARCH 18

Harry Powers executed in 1932

Harry Powers was a sadistic individual who took out ads to find unsuspecting women, take their money, and kill them. It was reported that he may have murdered 55 women. He was finally caught in Quiet Dell and convicted of the murders of Asta Eicher, her three children, and another woman, Dorothy Pressler. A book and movie titled *"The Night of the Hunter"* were loosely based upon his life. He was hanged and pronounced dead at 9:11 p.m.
Source: *"Pronounced Dead"* by C.J. Plogger

Harry Powers

MARCH 19

Shocking news

The wife of Warden M.Z. White was visiting family in Dayton, Ohio, when a report circulated that she had died. The warden immediately called Ohio, talked to his wife, and discovered she was alive and all was well.
Source: *Moundsville Weekly Echo*, March 19, 1915

Correctional officer intervention

Inmate John Larne stabbed another inmate, Henry Huston, in the back twice with scissors. If Correctional Officer Buck Lowery had not intervened, Larne probably would have killed Huston.
Source: *Moundsville Weekly Echo*, March 19, 1926

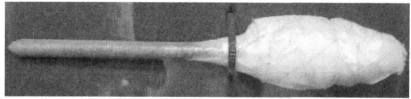

An inmate-made weapon

MARCH 20

Women's new building

A two-story building with a bath and laundry area was built for female inmates.
Source: *Moundsville Weekly Echo*, March 20, 1903

Hostages held

During a 1973 riot, five correctional officers were held hostage by 40 inmates. An inmate named Willie Hale was brutally murdered.
Source: *Moundsville Daily Echo*, March 20, 1973

1973 riot

MARCH 21

John Travis, Arnett Booth, and Orvil Adkins executed in 1938

John Travis, Arnett Booth, and Orvil Adkins kidnapped a minister named James Seder and held him for a ransom of $50,000. Seder was placed in an abandoned coal mine shaft and died of pneumonia after he was rescued. This was the second triple hanging of the penitentiary and these were the first men to be hanged after a federal law mandated if a kidnapping occurred and the victim died then the kidnapper would be put to death. The law was the result of the Lindbergh baby case. First, Travis and Adkins were hanged and both were pronounced dead at 9:14 p.m. Then Booth was hanged and pronounced dead at 9:48 p.m.

Source: *"Pronounced Dead"* by C.J. Plogger

John Travis   Arnett Booth   Orvil Adkins

MARCH 22

Poor aspirations

Two juveniles, Grover Littleton and Joseph Herman, were taken to reform school for their incorrigible behavior. They told people that they were "Peck's bad boys," a reference to prison Warden John Peck. It was also an allusion to the 1883 novel *"Peck's Bad Boy and His Pa"* by George Wilbur Peck, who served as Wisconsin's 17th governor.
Source: *Moundsville Weekly Echo*, March 22, 1907

Juvenile Correctional Complex in Pruntytown

MARCH 23

Lynching bill

A new bill passed on this day that stipulated if a West Virginia city or town lynched someone the offending municipality would be fined $5,000.
Source: *Moundsville Weekly Echo*, March 23, 1923

Busy chickens

On Easter 1940, the inmates ate 5,760 eggs.
Source: *Moundsville Daily Echo*, March 23, 1940

MARCH 24

Fire system installed

A fire extinguishing system was installed in the
penitentiary in 1905 for $19,700.
Source: *Moundsville Weekly Echo*, March 24, 1905

Fire system in Dining Hall

Tuberculosis

One hundred fifty-one inmates had tuberculosis in 1960.
Source: *Moundsville Daily Echo*, March 24, 1960

MARCH 25

Pen sewage system a mess

The penitentiary sewage system was almost condemned and shut down because it was pouring sewage into Middle Grave Creek, becoming a menace to the health and welfare of the community.
Source: *Moundsville Weekly Echo*, March 25, 1910

Sewage pipe along 98 Corridor

MARCH 26

Harry Burdette and Fred Painter executed in 1951

Harry Burdette and Fred Painter murdered Edward O'Brien after he refused to give them a carafe of wine he was carrying. They kicked him to death and earned the nickname "The Stomp Murderers." They were the first two inmates executed on "Old Sparky," the electric chair. Burdette was pronounced dead at 9:06 p.m., but Painter had to have a second charge course through his body because the first one did not kill him. He was finally pronounced dead at 9:22 p.m.
Source: *"Pronounced Dead"* by C.J. Plogger

Harry Burdette

Fred Painter

MARCH 27

Tom Ingram executed in 1954

When Zenobia Bigelow tried to break off her affair with Tom Ingram he became enraged and stabbed her to death with a butcher knife. The murder was witnessed by Zenobia's 7-year-old daughter, Melba, so Ingram killed her, too. He was electrocuted on "Old Sparky" and pronounced dead at 9:06 p.m.
Source: *"Pronounced Dead"* by C.J. Plogger

Tom Ingram

Closed down!

West Virginia Penitentiary closed in 1995 and many of the inmates were moved south to the Mount Olive Correctional Complex.
Source: *Moundsville Daily Echo*, March 27, 1995

Moundsville Daily Echo headline

MARCH 28

Inmate labor

In 1907, 275 inmates were contracted out to work nine hours a day making brooms, whips, and leather products. The factories had to pay for the power used and $300 a year to the penitentiary for rent.
Source: *Moundsville Weekly Echo*, March 28, 1907

Leather riveting machine in the penitentiary

MARCH 29

Habeas Corpus

Inmate Spencer Jones was released from the penitentiary because of a new law called Habeas Corpus. Habeas Corpus requires a person charged with a crime to be brought before a judge or a court and Jones had not been given due process.

Source: *Moundsville Weekly Echo*, March 29, 1907

Courthouse in Marshall County, West Virginia

MARCH 30

Andrew Brady executed in 1928

Andrew Brady sexually assaulted a 17-year-old girl at a picnic area in Moorefield. He confessed to the crime, but later denied it. He was married and had four children he left behind as he was hanged and pronounced dead at 9:13 p.m.

Source: *"Pronounced Dead"* by C.J. Plogger

Andrew Brady

James Chambers executed in 1945

James Chambers was serving time in the Huttonsville prison for murdering Mabel McIntyre. He slipped away from the prison and brutally murdered 73-year-old Lucy Ward. He had hidden in her barn and sexually assaulted her and then slit her throat. He was executed on Good Friday and pronounced dead at 9:16 p.m. No family members claimed his body.

Source: *"Pronounced Dead"* by C.J. Plogger

James Chambers

MARCH 31

Smashing stills

Emmeline Pankhurst was sent to the penitentiary for three years after she was convicted of inciting the malicious destruction of property. She was a temperance advocate and wanted to stop the production of alcohol.
Source: *Moundsville Weekly Echo*, March 31, 1913

Emmeline Pankhurst being arrested

Deadly drink

In 1943, four inmates died because they drank anti-freeze.
Source: *Moundsville Daily Echo*, March 31, 1943

Unwanted visitors

Marshall County resident Filander Simpson found two escaped inmates in his woods and talked them into turning themselves in.
Source: *Moundsville Daily Echo*, March 31, 1967

APRIL 1

Never executed

John Medley was convicted of murdering Neeley Shannon and received a death sentence. Medley lived under the death sentence for six years as his lawyers fought it and he was never executed.
Source: *Moundsville Weekly Echo*, April 1, 1910

Not good business

William Seabright was sentenced to serve 15 years in the penitentiary for killing his business partner, John Lubic, in Benwood. They owned a saloon and during a passionate dispute, Seabright fatally shot Lubic twice. Seabright was later paroled by Gov. William Glasscock.
Source: *Moundsville Weekly Echo*, April 1, 1904

Benwood, West Virginia

APRIL 2

Overcrowded

In 1914, there were 1,191 inmates in the penitentiary which caused severe overcrowding.
Source: *Moundsville Weekly Echo*, April 2, 1914

Bad hobos

Three hobos, James Baker, Fuzzy Rugan, and Young Clark, were convicted of murdering railroad operator Hutchinson. Baker claimed he was not involved and submitted several avowals of his innocence. He was a federal criminal, so he was moved from the West Virginia Penitentiary to Leavenworth Penitentiary in Kansas.
Source: *Moundsville Weekly Echo*, April 2, 1909

Leavenworth Penitentiary

Rough crime

William Hacker, 62, escaped from Camp Fair Chance in 1957. He was in prison because he murdered his housekeeper.
Source: *Moundsville Daily* Echo, April 2, 1957

APRIL 3

Needed marriage counseling

John Maley murdered his wife by poisoning her and served 20 years of his life sentence in the penitentiary. He was pardoned by Gov. William MacCorkle and did not die in prison.
Source: *Moundsville Weekly Echo*, April 3, 1896

Bones dug up

A skeleton was found when inmates were digging the foundation for the National Bed Factory in the North Yard of the penitentiary.
Source: *Moundsville Weekly Echo*, April 3, 1908

Elmer Bruner executed in 1959

Elmer Bruner became the last person executed in West Virginia. He was convicted of murdering 58-year-old Ruby Miller in Huntington, but he repeatedly and adamantly denied the crime. The electric chair, "Old Sparky" would end Bruner's life at 9:06 p.m. after 2,900 volts of electricity passed through his body.
Source: *"Pronounced Dead"* by C.J. Plogger

Elmer Bruner

APRIL 4

John Marshall and James Williams executed in 1913

This was one of the eight multiple executions that took place at the penitentiary. John Marshall murdered his wife, Minnie, after flying into a blind rage during an argument. James Williams murdered his 19-year-old wife, Rose, and her lover, Lucian Scott, after he discovered their illicit affair. The trap doors sprung open at 4:52 p.m. and Marshall was pronounced dead at 5:04 p.m. Williams was pronounced dead at 5:05 p.m.
Source: *"Pronounced Dead"* by C.J. Plogger

John Marshall   James Williams

Three amigos

Murderers Tomie Mollohan, Bobby Stacey, and David Williams all escaped on this date and were recaptured.
Source: *Moundsville Daily Echo*, April 4, 1988

APRIL 5

A lot of eggs

On Easter Sunday 1918, hungry inmates ate 2,880 eggs.
Source: *Moundsville Weekly Echo*, April 5, 1918

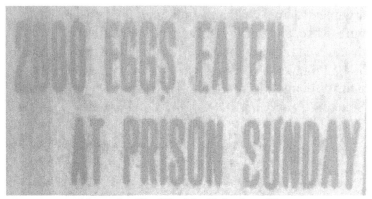

Moundsville Weekly Echo headline

APRIL 6

Suspicious fire

At 5 a.m., a fire raged through the south end of the Weaver, Birdall Factory in the penitentiary. The building and materials were insured for $12,000, but the damage was more than $15,000. The cause of the fire was unknown, but suspicious since there were no electric wires running through the building.

Source: *Moundsville Weekly Echo*, April 6, 1894

Whip that could have been made
in the Weaver, Birdall Factory

APRIL 7

Fresh water
Warden J.Z. Terrell wanted to put a water plant in the penitentiary. It would have required digging to a depth of 64 feet and would have supplied 4,000 gallons of fresh water an hour, but his plan was not implemented.
Source: *Moundsville Weekly Echo,* April 7, 1922

Hole of an old well at the penitentiary

APRIL 8

Escape from the mine

Inmates William Myers and Louis Sylvester escaped
from the prison mine. Myers was recaptured
immediately, but Sylvester stayed free for a few days
longer before he was recaptured.
Source: *Moundsville Weekly Echo*, April 8, 1927

West Virginia Penitentiary prison mine

Waited a long time

Clyde Peale was sentenced to death for murder in 1926,
but his sentence was not carried out. He was eventually
pardoned by Gov. Okey Patteson in 1949.
Source: *Moundsville Daily Echo*, April 8, 1949

APRIL 9

Very annoying

Inmates threw coal into the steam boiler to create smoke and irritate the correctional officers.
Source: *Moundsville Daily Echo*, April 9, 1957

Boiler in the West Virginia Penitentiary

APRIL 10

Defending his wife's honor

Inmate William Quills murdered inmate Charles Bennet by stabbing him in the neck with a knife. Quills claimed that Bennet slandered his wife, who was also a convict.
Source: *Moundsville Weekly Echo*, April 10, 1903

Drowns during escape

Austin Chipperfield, 26, was serving a three-year sentence for grand larceny, but decided he could not take it. He escaped, but drowned in the Ohio River. His body was recovered.
Source: *Moundsville Weekly Echo*, April 10, 1924

James Hewlett executed in 1951

Only 22, World War II veteran James Hewlett became extremely intoxicated and murdered taxi driver Julian Buie. Hewlett then robbed him and only received $6. He was executed on "Old Sparky" and pronounced dead at 9:08 p.m.
Source: *"Pronounced Dead"* by C.J. Plogger

James Hewlett

APRIL 11

Method of torture

The Weighing Machine would lift shackled inmates off the floor until they were dangling with just the tips of their toes reaching the ground. The blood of the inmates would pool in their lower extremities and then shoot upward, usually exiting through their fingertips. Countless inmates were either maimed or murdered by this horrific means of torture.
Source: *Wheeling Register*, April 11, 1886

Henry Sterling executed in 1913

Henry Sterling, 22, savagely murdered William Patterson by shooting him with a shotgun and then cutting off his head with a knife. Sterling had been renting an apartment from Patterson and while Sterling was intoxicated he started a fight with Patterson. Sterling was hanged and pronounced dead at 5:06 p.m.
Source: *"Pronounced Dead"* by C.J. Plogger

Henry Sterling

Not child's play

Fourteen-year-old, Tommy Williams was sentenced to life in the penitentiary because he killed 9-year-old David Powell.
Source: *Moundsville Daily Echo*, April 11, 1956

APRIL 12

Ingenious escape

Federal prisoner Green placed a dummy in his cell and hid in the North Yard until darkness set in. He then spliced two ladders together and scaled the walls to freedom. There is no record if he was recaptured.
Source: *Moundsville Weekly Echo*, April 12, 1901

Walls of the West Virginia Penitentiary

Hand in the cookie jar

West Virginia Department of Motor Vehicles Commissioner Jack Nuckols was sent to the penitentiary for falsifying expense accounts.
Source: *Moundsville Weekly Echo*, April 12, 1966

APRIL 13

Frank Pramesa executed in 1937

An affair between Frank Pramesa and Pearl Thames led them to concoct a plan to kill Pearl's husband, Louis Thames, to collect on an insurance policy. After Pramesa murdered his friend and co-worker, Pearl denied any involvement in the attack. She was tried for murder, but found not guilty. Pramesa was hanged and pronounced dead at 9:10 p.m.
Source: *"Pronounced Dead"* by C.J. Plogger

Frank Pramesa

Cramped quarters

John Hilley and Gerald Berger escaped from the penitentiary under the hood of a truck.
Source: *Moundsville Weekly Echo*, April 13, 1966

APRIL 14

Students visit pen

Sociology students from Bethany College, led by
Professor Newton Miller, toured the penitentiary to
observe abnormal behavior.
Source: *Moundsville Weekly Echo*, April 14, 1922

Bethany College

APRIL 15

Touring the pen

Visitors could come into the penitentiary to observe it six times a day in 1904. They were charged 25 cents for their excursion but could not view the gallows or death cells. The penitentiary received up to $10 a week for the visits. Source: *Moundsville Weekly Echo*, April 15, 1904

A penitentiary tour in 2018

New water tower

A new water tower was placed in the North Yard of the penitentiary to supply water for the inmates and prison. Source: *Moundsville Weekly Echo*, April 15, 1904

APRIL 16

Flu outbreak

An influenza epidemic in the prison was finally confined to 40 inmates after numbers of infected prisoners reached as high as 126. Twenty-five cases were severe enough that the inmates had to be hospitalized.
Source: *Moundsville Weekly Echo*, April 16, 1926

The big leagues

Escaped murderer Ronald Turney Williams was placed on the FBI's Top Ten Most Wanted List.
Source: *Moundsville Weekly Echo*, April 16, 1981

Ronald Williams' FBI Identification Order

APRIL 17

Oshel Gardner Jr. executed in 1953

Taxi driver Roy Jackson picked up Oshel Gardner Jr., who brutally murdered Jackson. Jackson was also the chief of the Point Pleasant Volunteer Fire Department and seven of its members were witnesses to Gardner's execution. Gardner was electrocuted on "Old Sparky" and pronounced dead at 9:05 p.m.
Source: *"Pronounced Dead"* by C.J. Plogger

Oshel Gardner Jr.

APRIL 18

New cells

One hundred-eighty iron cells were installed in the North Hall of the penitentiary. The work was completed by inmates, which saved money for the state.
Source: *Moundsville Weekly Echo*, April 18, 1903

Current North Hall

Influence of Mom

Gov. Henry D. Hatfield pardoned inmate E.L. Hopkins because Hopkins' mother grieved deeply and it was affecting her health.
Source: *Moundsville Weekly Echo*, April 18, 1913

APRIL 19

Early riot

In 1870, there was a riot during which two inmates were shot and one stabbed by another inmate.
Source: West Virginia Penitentiary Museum, *"Notebook No. 2"*

Harry Sawyer executed in 1926

An impulsive decision cost Harry Sawyer his life. Seeing Olive Amburgy walking down the street and wearing shiny jewelry, he knocked her down and took the jewelry from her. She fainted during the incident and Sawyer was convicted of rape and sentenced to death. Sawyer was hanged and pronounced dead at 5:11 p.m.
Source: *"Pronounced Dead"* by C.J. Plogger

Harry Sawyer

APRIL 20

Prison farm

Warden Charles E. Haddox reported that 50 bushels of onion sets, seven pounds of radish seeds, and two pounds of cabbage seeds had been planted. Three hundred bushels of potatoes had been harvested.
Source: *Moundsville Weekly Echo*, April 20, 1906

Camp Fair Chance

APRIL 21

Loyal girlfriend

A Huntington man was sent to the penitentiary for passing counterfeit money. His girlfriend loved him so much that she traveled from Huntington to be near him and stayed in Moundsville until his sentence was over 13 months later.
Source: *Moundsville Weekly Echo*, April 21, 1905

Huntington, West Virginia

Overcrowded

Inmate census was 1,492.
Source: *Moundsville Weekly Echo*, April 21, 1922

APRIL 22

Tall inmate

The tallest inmate in the penitentiary died. He had been sentenced to serve 18 months, but only survived four months in prison.
Source: *Moundsville Weekly Echo*, April 22, 1892

Most of the cells in the penitentiary measure 5 feet by 7 feet and the ceilings are 7 feet high

APRIL 23

Dumb decision

James Tate was sentenced to life in prison for murder. He was conditionally pardoned by Gov. William M.O. Dawson, but squandered the opportunity and was arrested after a fight. A gun was found on him, so he was sent back to the penitentiary to complete his life sentence.

Source: *Moundsville Weekly Echo*, April 23, 1909

West Virginia Penitentiary cell

APRIL 24

Not executed

Frank Panletta received the death penalty for murder, but his first execution date was postponed so that he could appeal. His appeal was successful and he escaped execution.
Source: *Moundsville Weekly Echo*, April 24, 1914

Death Chamber in the penitentiary

A long respite

Jay Watts escaped from the penitentiary and was not captured for 10 years.
Source: *Moundsville Weekly Echo*, April 24, 1936

APRIL 25

Hounds on the trail

Two convicts working on 10th Street in Moundsville escaped from their work crew. M.C. Morrison and his bloodhounds were called to search for them but were not successful. One of the young dogs refused to follow commands and was shot on the spot.
Source: *Moundsville Daily Echo*, April 25, 1907

Tenth Street in Moundsville

Getaway car

Eric Jackson and Billy Joe Gardner escaped by taking the car of a correctional officer.
Source: *Moundsville Weekly Echo*, April 25, 1972

APRIL 26

Jilted lover

Annie Hall was in love with Correctional Officer Rufus Childers, but her heart was broken when he returned from a vacation with a new bride. Disappointed and forlorn, Hall used a .32-caliber revolver to fire at Childers. The bullet tore through Childers' coat, but did not strike him. Hall was arrested but was set free after her trial.

Source: *Moundsville Weekly Echo*, April 26, 1901

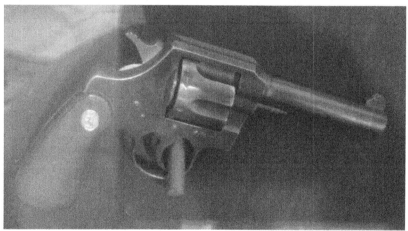

West Virginia Penitentiary Museum

APRIL 27

Angry inmate

Cecil Coleman ambushed fellow inmate Orville Rowsley in the Recreational Yard and stabbed him in the neck with a knife. Rowsley died later that evening. Coleman did not receive the death penalty for his horrific act. Source: *Moundsville Weekly Echo*, April 27, 1923

Recreational Yard in the penitentiary

APRIL 28

Coming home

An inmate escaped in 1918 and fled to Ohio where he continued his criminal behavior and ended up in a Buckeye State jail. He was tracked down by West Virginia authorities and brought back to the penitentiary in 1920.

Source: *Moundsville Weekly Echo*, April 28, 1920

APRIL 29

Bad business partners

Charles Forrest and Will Hyden were business partners in Keystone, selling moonshine. On this date in 1915, they got into a violent exchange and Forrest stabbed Hyden to death. Forrest was executed for the crime.
Source: *"Pronounced Dead"* by C.J. Plogger

Charles Forrest

APRIL 30

Hugh Bragg executed in 1920

Hugh Bragg lost both of his legs in a railroad accident, but this didn't deter him from pursuing a life of crime. Bragg killed Police Officer John Morris, 33, after he attempted to arrest Bragg following one of his illegal acts. Warden J.Z. Terrell had to limit the invitations to Bragg's hanging because many people wanted to see a man with no legs hanged.

Source: *"Pronounced Dead"* by C.J. Plogger

Hugh Bragg

MAY 1

Louis Young executed in 1902

Louis Young and Authur Kell got into a knock-down, drag-out brawl over the affection of a woman. Kell pounded Young into submission so he slinked off with his pride hurt, then returned with a rifle, and killed Kell. Source: *"Pronounced Dead"* by C.J. Plogger

Louis Young

Curious spectators

In 1945, 1,000 people stood on the Adena Burial Mound across the street from the penitentiary to watch an inferno inside the stone walls of the prison.
Source: *Moundsville Daily Echo*, May 1, 1945

Sneaky inmates

John Verton and Donald Williamson previously escaped from North Hall and tried again, but this time they were caught because correctional officers found the dummies they had placed in their bunks.
Source: *Moundsville Daily Echo*, May 1, 1979

MAY 2

Religious politics

Rev. D.W. Ruble started as chaplain for the penitentiary, but his choice was not approved by all and a petition was sent to the penitentiary board of directors against him. Its members did not listen to the complaints and he continued in his position.
Source: *Moundsville Weekly Echo*, May 2, 1902

Mount Rose Cemetery, Moundsville

Well-dressed inmate

Inmate James Goodwin was doing electrical work at the penitentiary and noticed that a correctional officer had left some of his clothes in the room. Goodwin took the clothes, scaled the wall with a ladder, and escaped. There was a $50 reward offered for his capture.
Source: *Moundsville Weekly Echo,* May 2, 1902

MAY 3

Different day job

An inmate, known only as Nay, was convicted and sentenced to four years in the penitentiary for stealing horses. It turned out he was a professionally trained doctor of medicine. He became the penitentiary doctor's assistant and was described as invaluable. After completing his sentence, he was picked up by a North Carolina prison guard to return him to a Tarheel State prison to finish a nine-year sentence for, yes, horse theft. Nay had escaped only to be captured in West Virginia.
Source: *Moundsville Weekly Echo,* May 3, 1895

Bountiful bouquets

There were 7,000 tulips in bloom in front of the penitentiary.
Source: *Moundsville Weekly Echo*, May 3, 1912

Hard Time

West Virginia Supreme Court Chief Justice Richard Neely said that 50 percent of the inmates did not need to be housed in cells and they could live and work in the community.
Source: *Moundsville Daily Echo*, May 3, 1985

Chief Justice Richard Neely

MAY 4

Monroe Payton executed in 1922

Monroe Payton was convicted of sexually assaulting a 9-year-old girl. It took the jury only 10 minutes to return a guilty verdict. When he arrived at the penitentiary under heavy guard, he was placed in solitary confinement. He went to the gallows without ever confessing his crime.
Source: *"Pronounced Dead"* by C.J. Plogger

Monroe Payton

Cramped

In 1923, there were 1,683 inmates with space for only 800.
Source: *Moundsville Weekly Echo*, May 4, 1923

Crowded death cells

Five men, James Aiello, Philip Connizaro, Dick Ferri, Nic Salamante, and Sam Muratore, all murderers, were placed in the death cells. Aiello murdered a store clerk, but was not executed. Connizaro, Ferri, and Salamante were executed in the first triple hanging at the penitentiary.
Source: *Moundsville Weekly Echo*, May 4, 1923

MAY 5

Needing mental health

Jackson Jeffers, Church Combs, and Brown Lipscomb were adjudged insane and were ordered to the Weston State Hospital as soon as arrangements could be made.
Source: *Moundsville Weekly Echo*, May 5, 1905

Weston State Hospital

'Interesting description'

In 1910, a newspaper described the penitentiary as a point of interest.
Source: *Moundsville Weekly Echo*, May 5, 1910

Sad situation

The mother of Benton Amos was widowed when Benton was just a few years old and she asked a neighborhood family to take care of Benton for a short time until she could get back on her feet. When Benton was 5 years old, the neighborhood family took him and moved away. Benton's mother did not see him for another 20 years when she discovered that he was serving time in the penitentiary. She and a sister visited with Benton and were traveling to see the governor about Benton's release when he died from consumption.
Source: *Moundsville Weekly Echo*, May 5, 1916

MAY 6

Filling up quickly

In 1892, there were 338 inmates.
Source: *Moundsville Weekly Echo*, May 6, 1892

Can't keep me

George Harrington escaped twice from the penitentiary
and received an additional five-year sentence.
Source: *Moundsville Weekly Echo*, May 6, 1927

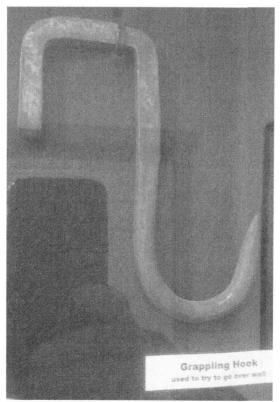

West Virginia Penitentiary Museum

MAY 7

Good report

Warden Joseph E. Matthews reported to Gov. William E. Glasscock that all was running well at the penitentiary. Source: *Moundsville Weekly Echo*, May 7, 1909

West Virginia Penitentiary

MAY 8

Not a happy inmate

Convicted murderer Jesse Briggs went berserk in the North Yard and started throwing bricks at guards. Officer Bloyd shot in Briggs' direction four times to persuade him to stop. Acting Warden C.G. Dawson ran to the yard and shot Briggs. The mayhem took place at 7:25 a.m.
Source: *Moundsville Weekly Echo*, May 8, 1908

Overcrowded

In 1925, there were 1,680 inmates while there was only space for 800.
Source: *Moundsville Weekly Echo*, May 8, 1925

Old-time postcard of the penitentiary

MAY 9

First double execution in 1902

John Mooney and Frank Friday were the first multiple execution. They broke into 70-year-old James Hervey's home to rob him, but instead murdered him. Hervey had recently sold property for $11,000 and Mooney and Friday were after the money. Years later, a carpenter remodeling the Hervey home found $11,000 hidden under one of the floorboards. While he was awaiting execution, Mooney escaped from the penitentiary and shot and killed Henry Peter. Mooney was immediately captured and returned to face his death sentence.
Source: *"Pronounced Dead"* by C.J. Plogger

John Mooney

Frank Friday

Walter Crabtree executed in 1930

Seeking revenge on Henry Inskeep, Walter Crabtree went to the courthouse in Romney and killed him. Blinded by rage, Crabtree also murdered another nemesis, Benjamin Miller. Unfortunately, there was an innocent bystander named Edward Malcolm who was killed as well. Crabtree was hanged and pronounced dead at 9:08 p.m.
Source: *"Pronounced Dead"* by C.J. Plogger

Walter Crabtree

MAY 10

Bad fall

At 8:30 a.m., one of the prison's oldest correctional officers, F.W. Baldwin, fell off a wagon loaded with corn at Camp Fair Chance. One of the wheels rolled over his head, causing a deep gash on his scalp that bled excessively. Baldwin survived his injuries and returned to work.
Source: *Moundsville Weekly Echo*, May 10, 1912

Moving on

Warden Samuel Hawk left Moundsville for the final time as his term of duty was over. He remarked he was much wiser for having been the warden for the penitentiary.
Source: *Moundsville Weekly Echo*, May 10, 1910

WARDEN SAM A. HAWK.

Warden Sam Hawk

MAY 11

Horrible crime

On May 11, 1928, Lawrence Fike entered a grocery store in Preston County to steal items. As he was leaving the store, the owner, Elroy Leonard, walked in and they exchanged small talk, even joking together. Leonard then went to a nearby field to milk his cows. Fike followed him because he thought that Leonard knew what he had done and would report him to authorities. As Leonard was milking a cow, Fike grabbed a piece of wood and twice clubbed Leonard over the head. Leonard's life blood spurted quickly from his skull. Fike was executed for his crime less than three months later.
Source: *Pronounced Dead* by C.J. Plogger

Lawrence Fike

MAY 12

Closed on Sunday

The Logan County sheriff needed to bring six convicts to the penitentiary, but it did not receive inmates on Sundays so the prisoners were securely housed in the Logan County Jail until Monday morning.
Source: *Moundsville Weekly Echo*, May 12, 1893

Free for a while

Two inmates cut holes in the top of their North Hall cells and escaped.
Source: *Moundsville Weekly Echo*, May 12, 1922

North Hall from the North Yard

MAY 13

Getting full

The penitentiary housed more than 1,000 inmates for the first time in 1904.
Source: Moundsville *Weekly Echo*, May 13, 1904

James Blount executed in 1932

James Blount's wife left him for another man and he was crushed. He confronted his wife's new beau and they engaged in a violent altercation in Tennessee. After the fight in a pool room, Blount moved to West Virginia, but Jesse Meeks, the man who Blount fought, followed him to the Mountain State to continue the confrontation. Meeks and another Tennessean soundly beat Blount by breaking two bottles over his head, causing him to sink into unconsciousness. Five days later, Blount found Meeks and shot him two times with a shotgun. Blount was hanged and pronounced dead at 9:14 p.m.
Source: *"Pronounced Dead"* by C.J. Plogger

James Blount

MAY 14
Too much money

Warden M.Z. White started buying potatoes instead of growing them on the prison farm because it cost more to harvest them than to purchase them.
Source: *Moundsville Weekly Echo*, May 14, 1915

Helping the kids

The labor of more than 12 inmates was used for a good cause when they built a new city playground in Moundsville for children.
Source: *Moundsville Weekly Echo*, May 14, 1926

Playground in Moundsville

Good reason?

Morris Billups escaped from the penitentiary and had a unique reason for fleeing. His defense: the living conditions were so bad at the penitentiary that he simply could not stay there.
Source: *Moundsville Daily Echo*, May 14, 1983

MAY 15

Get rid of it

The R.J. McFadden family owned the large Adena mound across the street from the penitentiary and in 1908 they were seriously considering tearing it down to build homes. They chose not to raze it and R.J. McFadden transferred ownership to the State of West Virginia in 1909. Gov. William E. Glasscock put Warden Joseph E. Matthews in charge of its maintenance and upkeep. Source: *Moundsville Weekly Echo*, May 15, 1908

Adena Burial Mound in Moundsville

MAY 16

Venture capitalists

Since the penitentiary was scheduled to be shut down because of "cruel and unusual punishment" and inmates were to be transferred to other correctional facilities, businessmen wanted to turn the prison into a mall.
Source: *Moundsville Daily Echo*, May 16, 1991

Would it have two or three floors?

MAY 17

Deadly drink

Inmates Wayne Short and Jonathan Jenkins went to the hospital for drinking prison whiskey. It was not a safe batch and they died the next day.
Source: *Moundsville Daily Echo*, May 17, 1970

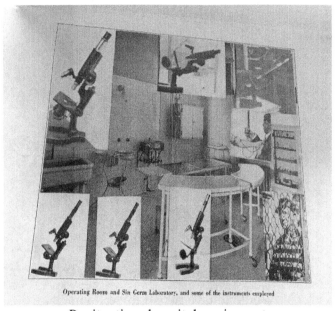

Operating Room and Sin Germ Laboratory, and some of the instruments employed

Penitentiary hospital equipment
Found in *"The Trail of the Dead Years"* by Earl Dudding

MAY 18

No more executions

West Virginia abolished the death penalty in 1965 after 85 hangings and nine electrocutions in the penitentiary. Source: *"Pronounced Dead"* by C.J. Plogger

Generator for "Old Sparky"

MAY 19

A lot of sewing in 1899

Two factories inside the penitentiary, Klee Co. and Kraft Co., had the most sewing machines in Marshall County. The Klee Co. had 160 sewing machines and the Kraft Co. had 140 machines.
Source: *Moundsville Weekly Echo*, May 19, 1899

Early prison reformer

Earl Dudding, early prison reformer, arrived at the penitentiary for murdering his uncle.
Source: *Moundsville Journal*, May 19, 1910

Earl Dudding in front of the Wheel

MAY 20

A great deal of authority

A legislative act gave prison officials the authority to determine the length of a convict's sentence. The warden and board of directors could impose either a minimum or maximum penalty after a conviction.
Source: *Moundsville Weekly Echo*, May 20, 1904

Not handling conflict well

Harry Allman received a one- to five-year sentence in the penitentiary after he shot and killed two horses owned by W.B. Riggs. Allman and Riggs were entangled in an argument over the condition of the fence separating their land.
Source: *Moundsville Weekly Echo*, May 20, 1924

Deadly fall

Inmate Hugh Miller died after he fell from a third-floor window of the prison.
Source: *Moundsville Daily Echo*, May 20, 1946

West Virginia Penitentiary

MAY 21

Overcrowded

In 1925, there were 1,700 inmates in the penitentiary.
Source: *Moundsville Weekly Echo*, May 21, 1925

Pleading not guilty

Henry Jackson murdered Correctional Officer Earl
Langfitt on March 11, 1926, and pleaded not guilty.
Jackson was executed later for the crime.
Source: *Moundsville Weekly Echo*, May 21, 1926

Website listing officers who died in the line of duty

MAY 22

Women coming to the penitentiary

The building that would house the women was nearly completed in May 1903.
Source: *Moundsville Weekly Echo*, May 22, 1903

Low pay

In 1903, correctional officers at the penitentiary were paid $1.65 a day for their first year and $2 their second year. After five years of service, pay rose to $2.25 per day.
Source: *Moundsville Weekly Echo*, May 22, 1903

Correctional Officer Maggie Gray

MAY 23

Farm escape

James Nay escaped from the prison farm while serving three years for horse stealing. He was caught less than a month later on June 20.
Source: *Moundsville Weekly Echo*, May 23, 1902

Area where Nay escaped

MAY 24

Prison farm

In 1903, Warden Charles E. Haddox bought 130 acres of land for $18,000 to be used as a farm for the prison. Source: *Moundsville Daily Echo*, May 24, 1907

Prison farm

MAY 25

No draft dodgers

West Virginia penitentiary inmates between the ages of 21 and 31 were required to register for the draft during World War I. It was unlikely they would have been called unless there had been an extraordinary necessity. Source: *Moundsville Weekly Echo*, May 25, 1917

Young men signing up for the draft

MAY 26

Arson

John Cavanaugh was sentenced to five years in the penitentiary because he burned down a building in order to get the insurance money. He lived in the town of Cameron, which is less than 20 miles from Moundsville.
Source: *Moundsville Weekly Echo*, May 26, 1922

Cameron, West Virginia

Too much sugar

John Woodstoff was sentenced to two years in the penitentiary for having a moonshine still in the basement of the house he was leasing. He was caught because people noticed that he had purchased several hundred pounds of sugar, a key ingredient in moonshine.
Source: *Moundsville Weekly Echo*, May 26, 1926

MAY 27

America's game

In 1920, the West Virginia Terriers, the inmate baseball team, started playing teams from outside the penitentiary.
Source: *Moundsville Weekly Echo*, May 27, 1920

Area of former baseball field

Overcrowded

There were 1,999 inmates in the penitentiary.
Source: *Moundsville Weekly Echo*, May 27, 1927

Unusual moonshiner

Mary Kelley was sentenced to three years in the penitentiary for the felony of producing moonshine. Judge Morris pronounced the sentence and said, "Women in this country are on equal footing with men and there will be no distinction in this case."
Source: *Moundsville Weekly Echo*, May 27, 1927

MAY 28

No unions

Frank Corich was sentenced to 10 years in the penitentiary for conspiracy in urging coal miners to strike. Corich was a Russian who lived in Glen Dale.
Source: *Moundsville Weekly Echo*, May 28, 1925

Striking coal miners

Not using his head

William Lelangovich was paroled from the penitentiary, but he returned very shortly. He was found to have a "liberal supply of moonshine on his person for future use." He would not have been rearrested if he had not been so visibly drunk in public.
Source: *Moundsville Weekly Echo*, May 28, 1925

MAY 29

Nicer appearance

The front steps of the North Administration building were lengthened, which added greatly to the appearance of the building.
Source: *Moundsville Weekly Echo*, May 29, 1896

New front steps

MAY 30

Celebration

In 1907, the inmates of the penitentiary enjoyed a vaudeville program and the band made them feel as if it were a holiday.
Source: *Moundsville Weekly Echo*, May 30, 1907

Where the bandstand once stood

MAY 31

New kind of entertainment

In 1912, the inmates enjoyed an innovative form of entertainment: picture shows, better known today as movies.
Source: *Moundsville Weekly Echo*, May 31, 1912

Penitentiary gym where movies were shown

JUNE 1

Marching along

The prison band played and marched in the 1943
Memorial Day parade in Moundsville.
Source: *Moundsville Daily Echo*, June 1, 1943

West Virginia Penitentiary band

JUNE 2

Fighting over office

Gov. William M.O. Dawson appointed the members of the prison board of directors and there was "a great deal of rivalry" among several prospective candidates. People wanted to serve on the board because it was an influential position and paid very well.
Source: *Moundsville Weekly Echo*, June 2, 1905

Gov. William M.O. Dawson

JUNE 3

Open door policy

On this date in 1949, 14 inmates escaped from the penitentiary.
Source: *Moundsville Daily Echo*, June 3, 1949

Shotguns in West Virginia Penitentiary Museum

JUNE 4

Pardoned of heinous crime

An inmate, known only as Yates, was convicted and condemned to death for sadistically murdering a 14-year-old girl. He would receive respites and eventually be pardoned by the governor. He was not executed.
Source: *Moundsville Weekly Echo*, June 4, 1909

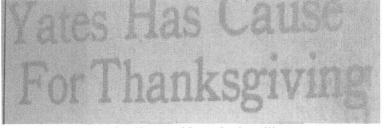

Moundsville Weekly Echo headline

JUNE 5

Wilfred Davis executed in 1903

Wilfred Davis' father was a Methodist minister, but he began to make bad choices as a juvenile and spent time in the reform school in Pruntytown. Davis was being taken to jail for being drunk and disorderly when he shot Elkins Police Chief Page Marstiller through his temple leading to his death five hours later. Davis escaped from the Elkins jail, but was recaptured the next morning. He was hanged and pronounced dead at 5:50 p.m.
Source: *"Pronounced Dead"* by C.J. Plogger

Wilfred Davis

Wall knocked down

A wall separating the female inmates from the male inmates collapsed in 1914 when a huge storm swept through the penitentiary.
Source: *Moundsville Weekly Echo*, June 5, 1914

Eugene Linger executed in 1958

Eugene Linger was a veteran of World War II and served twice in the U.S. Navy, but did not do well in the civilian world. He viciously murdered William White on Dec. 8, 1956. Linger was electrocuted on "Old Sparky" on June 5, 1958, and pronounced dead at 7:46 p.m.
Source: *"Pronounced Dead"* by C.J. Plogger

Eugene Linger

JUNE 6

John Hix executed in 1913

John Hix, 26, was deeply in love with Mary Thompson and wanted to marry her, but she spurned his affections because she was widowed and did not want any other male relationships. Hix flew into a frenzy and murdered her with a handgun. He was hanged and pronounced dead at 5:17 p.m.
Source: *"Pronounced Dead"* by C.J. Plogger

John Hix

Overcrowded

In 1913, there were 1,151 inmates in the penitentiary.
Source: *Moundsville Weekly Echo*, June 6, 1913

JUNE 7

Filling up

In 1895, there were 516 inmates in the penitentiary.
Source: *Moundsville Weekly Echo*, June 7, 1895

Inmates walking in lockstep

JUNE 8

Road crew

In 1906, the inmates paved 8th Street in Moundsville.
Source: *Moundsville Weekly Echo*, June 8, 1906

Last word

In Warden J.Z. Terrell's final report before he left the
penitentiary, he wrote that the prison was self-sufficient.
Source: *Moundsville Weekly Echo*, June 8, 1923

Top Ten Most Wanted fugitive caught

Ronald Turney Williams, escaped convicted murderer,
was shot by FBI agents at the George Washington Hotel
in New York City and taken into custody. Williams
eventually was taken to Arizona and received the death
penalty for the murder of John Bunchek. He was not
executed and is still imprisoned in West Virginia.
Source: *"Wayward Genius"* by C.J. Plogger

RONALD TURNEY WILLIAMS

JUNE 9

Didn't stay out of trouble

Burell Forgey was an inmate at the penitentiary and received a conditional pardon from Gov. William E. Glasscock. But two years later, Forgey committed a felony in Kentucky and was sentenced to a penitentiary in the Bluegrass State. After serving his time there, Warden Joseph E. Matthews picked him up and brought him back to the West Virginia Penitentiary since his pardon had been contingent upon him not getting into any more trouble.
Source: *Moundsville Weekly Echo*, June 9, 1910

Gov. William E. Glasscock

JUNE 10

Second correctional officer death

Correctional Officer A.H. Evans, 56, worked at the penitentiary for 15 years. He had a stroke at the Wheel, the spinning entrance into the penitentiary, shortly after starting his shift at 6 a.m. He was the second West Virginia Penitentiary correctional officer to die in service.

Source: *Moundsville Weekly Echo*, June 10, 1927

The Wheel

JUNE 11

Baptisms

Two condemned inmates, Mat Jarrell and William Stewart, were baptized by prison chaplain B.M. Spurr in the prison fountain in the presence of Warden M.Z. White and Capt. J.E. Boyd.
Source: *Moundsville Weekly Echo*, June 11, 1915

Reverend B.M. Spurr's headstone

JUNE 12

Protection

A U.S. marshal brought several federal prisoners to Moundsville to keep them safe and to ensure they would not escape.
Source: *Moundsville Weekly Echo*, June 12, 1896

U.S. marshal badge

Typhoid Fever

Inmates working on a road crew were hospitalized because they became very ill during an outbreak of typhoid fever.
Source: *Moundsville Weekly Echo*, June 12, 1914

JUNE 13

Perry Christian executed in 1902

Perry Christian and George Dent became entangled in a brutal brawl and Christian pulled a handgun out and fatally shot Dent. Some witnesses stated the shooting was in self-defense, while others said that Christian shot Dent in "the most cold-blooded manner." Christian was hanged and pronounced dead at 5:22 p.m.
Source: *"Pronounced Dead"* by C.J. Plogger

Perry Christian

JUNE 14

Theodore Carr executed in 1929

Theodore Carr and his estranged wife, Maggie Carr, had a deadly argument about land. After their separation, Maggie went to live with her brother, Lock Sharp, on an adjoining farm. Carr murdered Lock, 27, and then chased Maggie. When he caught her, they engaged in yet another intense argument and Carr shot her several times at point-blank range. He was hanged and pronounced dead at 9:07 p.m.

Source: *"Pronounced Dead"* by C.J. Plogger

Theodore Carr

JUNE 15

Overcrowded

In 1923, there were 1,675 inmates at the prison.
Source: *Moundsville Weekly Echo*, June 15, 1923

High honor

Robert Ashworth, penitentiary doctor, became the
president of the Association of West Virginia Doctors.
Source: *Moundsville Weekly Echo*, June 15, 1923

Dr. Robert Ashworth

JUNE 16

Overturned

Inmates Arthur Carver and Obrey Reed had their convictions overturned because they did not have lawyers at their trials.
Source: *Moundsville Daily Echo*, June 16, 1965

Representing himself

Charles Coon was the first inmate to represent himself in court. His trial started earlier in January.
Source: *Moundsville Weekly Echo*, June 16, 1918

Headline from *Moundsville Weekly Echo*

JUNE 17

Improving the appearance

Local painters finished wall papering and painting the fourth floor of the penitentiary's administration building, which was used for the warden's residence.
Source: *Moundsville Weekly Echo*, June 17, 1910

Not a nice lady

Ira Knight was sentenced to serve five years in the penitentiary because she assaulted Lula Jones. This was the lengthiest sentence given to a woman for this type of crime.
Source: *Moundsville Weekly Echo*, June 17, 1914

JUNE 18

A really bad lady

Ada Cross was a rough female inmate. In her first stint at the penitentiary, she stabbed Lottie Hawkins with a pair of scissors, which killed her instantly. Because of her bad behavior, Cross was sent back to Washington, D.C., because she was a federal prisoner. But officials there could not handle her, so, after two years, she was returned to the penitentiary.
Source: *Moundsville Weekly Echo*, June 18, 1909

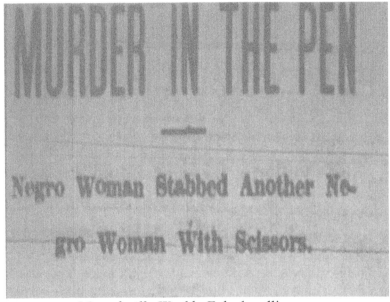

Moundsville Weekly Echo headline

JUNE 19

Frank Hyer executed in 1931

Frank Hyer was described as a "mean drunk." Overwhelmed by the stress of running a restaurant, he snapped while intoxicated and brutally beat his wife. After he repeatedly pummeled her, he struck her with a stick until she died. When he was hanged, he was decapitated.

Source: *"Pronounced Dead"* by C.J. Plogger

Frank Hyer

JUNE 20

Full of bologna

The Morris and Co. business received a contract to
supply bologna to the penitentiary for $3.75 per barrel.
Source: *Moundsville Weekly Echo*, June 20, 1908

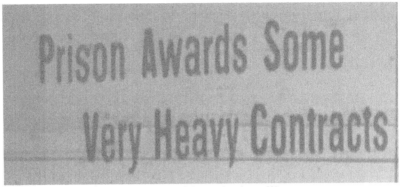

Moundsville Weekly Echo headline

JUNE 21

Not politically correct

A female convict brought to the penitentiary was described as a "robust wench of stout build."
Source: *Moundsville Weekly Echo*, June 21, 1901

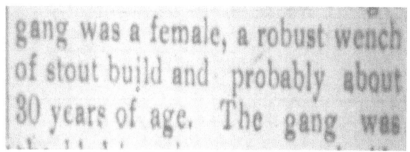

gang was a female, a robust wench of stout build and probably about 30 years of age. The gang was

Moundsville Weekly Echo article

JUNE 22

Hot place

On June 22, 1923, it was 105 degrees in the penitentiary.
Source: *Moundsville Weekly Echo*, June 22, 1923

Fan in North Hall

JUNE 23

'Belly-ache'

Inmate W.H. Edwards was serving a 10-year sentence for grand larceny. He served three years and two months, but was pardoned by Gov. George W. Atkinson because of failing health. Prison officials nicknamed Edwards "Belly-ache" because of his constant complaints.
Source: *Moundsville Weekly Echo*, June 23, 1897

Gov. George W. Atkinson

Mail block

Twenty-three families were mad because penitentiary officials placed a fence at the southeast corner of the prison, which shut off the path of the mailman. That forced residents to travel to the Post Office to pick up their mail instead of having it delivered.
Source: *Moundsville Weekly Echo*, June 23, 1905

JUNE 24

Almost executed

Al Moore was convicted of first-degree murder and almost received the death penalty. Eleven of the 12 jurors wanted him to receive it, but one adamantly disagreed, so he received a life sentence instead. There was discussion whether the killing was a murder for hire because he had $117.77 in his pocket when he was arrested.
Source: *Moundsville Weekly Echo*, June 24, 1914

Electrical coils for generator of "Old Sparky"

JUNE 25

Willie Beckner executed in 1937

Willie Beckner broke into the house of his neighbor, Joseph Page, intending to rob him. Beckner did not find any money, but did take a shotgun and later found Page and murdered him with his own weapon. Beckner was hanged and pronounced dead at 8:56 p.m.
Source: *"Pronounced Dead"* by C.J. Plogger

Willie Beckner

JUNE 26

Presidential candidate

Eugene Debs ran unsuccessfully four times for the presidency of the United States as a candidate for the Socialist Party of America. He was imprisoned for violating the Espionage Act for speeches he made while running for office. He was imprisoned in the West Virginia Penitentiary starting in April 1919 and was transferred to the Atlanta Federal Penitentiary in 1919 on this date.
Source: *Moundsville Weekly Echo*, June 26, 1919

Eugene Debs

Shooting in North Hall

Twelve inmates refused to go back into their cells after their recreation time so correctional officers in riot gear confronted them. The inmates threw a volatile liquid at the correctional officers and they opened fire. Four inmates were injured, including Marcus Cockerham, who was paralyzed.
Source: *Wheeling Intelligencer*, June 26, 1986

JUNE 27

Heinous crime

In 1904, George Williams sexually assaulted 20-year-old Laura Knade. Williams was going to kill the young schoolteacher, but she begged for her life and he allowed her to live. She then ran to a nearby farm and reported the crime. Williams was later executed.
Source: *"Pronounced Dead"* by C.J. Plogger

George Williams

JUNE 28

Byzantine Hartman executed in 1940

Byzantine Hartman was a cruel man who was once arrested for viciously beating his mother. Upshur County Policeman Wilbur Grubb was serving a warrant for Hartman, who murdered him with a shotgun. Hartman was hanged and pronounced dead at 9:12 p.m.
Source: *"Pronounced Dead"* by C.J. Plogger

Byzantine Hartman

JUNE 29

Stone cells

In 1906, all the cells of the penitentiary were fashioned of stone. Later that year, they were replaced with steel cells. With only 226 stone cells, there were 1,260 inmates in the penitentiary, causing great overcrowding.
Source: *Moundsville Weekly Echo*, June 29, 1906

Cells in South Hall

JUNE 30

Extremely overcrowded

In 1930, there were 840 cells and 2,378 inmates housed at the penitentiary.
Source: *Moundsville Weekly Echo*, June 30, 1930

Inmates walking in cell block

JULY 1

Larry Fudge executed in 1958

Larry Fudge was an honor student in Huntington and well liked. He grew up with the two sons of Inez Booth whose husband was a city councilman. On Jan. 4, 1958, Fudge forced Inez from her home then stabbed her repeatedly with a knife and raped her. As she was dying, she named Fudge as her attacker and he later confessed to the crime. He was executed on "Old Sparky" and pronounced dead at 10:15 p.m.
Source: *"Pronounced Dead"* by C.J. Plogger

UDGE, LARRY PAUL #41721

Larry Fudge

JULY 2

Foolish words

The parole of Kirk Piersol was revoked because he publicly bragged about how he "fleeced the yaps and hosiers of Moundsville." This comment did not please law enforcement officials and he was returned to serve the rest of his sentence in the penitentiary.
Source: *Moundsville Weekly Echo*, July 2, 1909

Will Stewart and Will Thomas executed in 1915

During his arrest by Roncerverte Police Chief George Shires, Will Stewart aggressively resisted, took Chief Shires' handgun, and fatally shot the chief during the struggle. Stewart was hanged and pronounced dead at 5:36 p.m.
Source: *"Pronounced Dead"* by C.J. Plogger

Will Thomas did not believe his 22-year old wife, Frieda, was faithful, so in the midst of a heated argument, Thomas shot her with a handgun. Thomas was hanged and pronounced dead at 5:36 p.m.
Source: *"Pronounced Dead"* by C.J. Plogger

Will Stewart   Will Thomas

JULY 3

Warden in trouble

Sam Hawk served as warden at Moundsville and then became warden of the Atlanta Federal Penitentiary. There he was investigated by U.S. Rep. Leonidas F. Livingston for tampering with a report about the Atlanta prison and was fired.
Source: *Moundsville Weekly Echo*, July 3, 1903

Atlanta Federal Penitentiary

New well

A new water well descending to 30 feet was dug at the prison farm.
Source: *Moundsville Weekly Echo*, July 3, 1908

JULY 4

Celebration

The penitentiary hosted "open houses" during which families of the inmates could come into the South Yard and spend time with the inmates. Inmates grilled hot dogs and hamburgers and had games for the kids to play. Source: Personal Interview with former West Virginia Penitentiary Correctional Officer Chuck Ghent

South Yard

JULY 5

Tailor factory

The Detter and Hughs Tailor factory was built within the walls of the penitentiary.
Source: *Moundsville Weekly Echo*, July 5, 1895

A lot of parolees

In 1935, Gov. Herman G. Kump paroled 47 inmates.
Source: *Moundsville Daily Echo*, July 5, 1935

Gov. Herman Kump

JULY 6

Relocating

When Marshall Watson was released from the penitentiary after serving his time for burglary, a deputy sheriff was waiting for him outside. He took Watson to a Kentucky prison to serve a term for a burglary conviction in the Bluegrass State.
Source: *Moundsville Weekly Echo*, July 6, 1917

Another Celebration

During a flag-raising celebration at the penitentiary, the inmates played baseball, ran races, and boxed.
Source: *Moundsville Weekly Echo*, July 6, 1928

Boxing at the penitentiary

JULY 7

Overcrowded

In 1922, there were 1,620 inmates at the penitentiary.
Source: *Moundsville Weekly Echo*, July 7, 1922

Steam turbine

A giant steam turbine was installed at the penitentiary in 1937 to produce electrical power.
Source: *Moundsville Daily Echo*, July 7, 1937

Prison steam turbine

JULY 8

Starved to death

Tony Gradison was a 32-year-old inmate who had received a life sentence, but did not want to serve it. He starved himself and, while every effort was made to save him, he died.
Source: *Moundsville Weekly Echo*, July 8, 1921

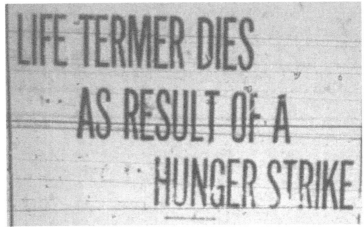

Headline from *Moundsville Weekly Echo*

Donating blood

During a drive to collect blood for use by the military during the Korean War, 358 inmates made donations.
Source: *Moundsville Daily Echo*, July 8, 1952

JULY 9

Mat Jarrell executed in 1915

Mat Jarrell, who had only one leg, was in love with a woman, but Edward Ratcliff loved her, too. Jarrell wanted to eliminate the competition so he killed Ratcliff. While Deputy Sheriff Silas Nantz was arresting Jarrell, he killed the officer as well. There were only 18 witnesses in the execution chamber.
Source: *"Pronounced Dead"* by C.J. Plogger

Mat Jarrell

JULY 10

Silas Jones executed in 1914

Silas Jones and his wife, Prudential, had a rocky marriage during which he constantly thought she was unfaithful. He was overcome with jealousy and murdered her with a shotgun. He was hanged and pronounced dead at 5:11 p.m.
Source: *"Pronounced Dead"* by C.J. Plogger

Silas Jones

JULY 11

Free!

Four inmates escaped by sawing through the bars of a basement window. Their absence was noticed at the 8 p.m. count.
Source: *Moundsville Weekly Echo*, July 11, 1919

Basement window bars

Angry inmates

Inmates were infuriated on this day in 1990 because a new law was enacted that permitted their phone conversations to be recorded and listened to by prison authorities.
Source: *Moundsville Daily Echo*, July 11, 1990

JULY 12

Unique event

A dance was held for a small number of inmates in 1895.
Music was provided from several instruments including a
harp. Four female chaperones carefully watched the
dancers.
Source: *Moundsville Weekly Echo*, July 12, 1895

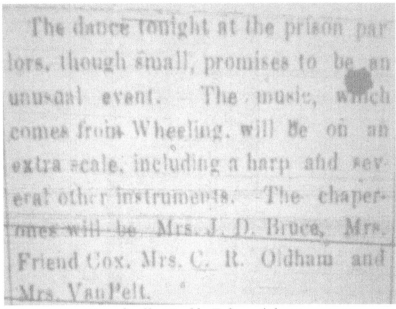

Moundsville Weekly Echo article

JULY 13

New barn

A barn was built on the south side of the penitentiary, replacing an old stable.
Source: *Moundsville Weekly Echo*, July 13, 1906

Prison barn

Not so quick

When Allen Thomas was released from the penitentiary, he was met by a law enforcement officer at the front door. Thomas was promptly taken back into custody to face charges from another state.
Source: *Moundsville Weekly Echo*, July 13, 1917

JULY 14

High fence

In 1953, a high, wire fence was placed in front of the old part of the penitentiary.
Source: *Moundsville Daily Echo*, July 14, 1953

West Virginia Penitentiary fencing

JULY 15

Disaster

West Virginia Institution Commissioner J. Donald Clark said the penitentiary was a "complete disaster."
Source: *Moundsville Daily Echo*, July 15, 1970

West Virginia Penitentiary

JULY 16

New cells

In 1897, North Hall was extended and 136 more cells were installed, costing $8,150.
Source: *Moundsville Weekly Echo*, July 16, 1897

North Hall

Late for a funeral

Inmate Marshall Henry escaped from the penitentiary after he ran away from a correctional officer while being escorted to a funeral. He was free for 18 years.
Source: *Moundsville Daily Echo*, July 16, 1960

JULY 17

Bad day at the penitentiary

With an execution scheduled later that day, inmate Oscar Pipps sneaked up on inmate William Banks and plunged a dagger into his heart, killing him. Pipps was described as the "most treacherous prisoner and worst man in the penitentiary."
Source: *Moundsville Weekly Echo*, July 17, 1908

Frank Johnson executed in 1908

Frank Johnson murdered Beulah Martin with a handgun during a lover's quarrel. In the days prior to his execution, he confessed to murdering four other people. These crimes made Johnson West Virginia's first serial killer. Johnson was hanged and pronounced dead at 5:22 p.m.
Source: *"Pronounced Dead"* by C.J. Plogger

Frank Johnson

JULY 18

Wrestling at the penitentiary

Moundsville residents could enter the South Yard of the prison to watch wrestling matches among the inmates. Some of the inmates wrestling names were Hose Nose, The Black Knight, and The Masked Marvel.
Source: *Moundsville Daily Echo*, July 18, 1964

South Wagon Gate entrance into South Yard

JULY 19

Sad ending

Inmate Jerry Moss committed suicide at the penitentiary by using a rope made out of his socks.
Source: *Moundsville Daily Echo*, July 19, 1982

M Block of New Wall

JULY 20

Hungry for blackberries

Four inmates serving time on the prison farm trespassed on W.G. Maxwell's land to steal blackberries. Maxwell was able to capture one of them as they fled, but the other three got away.
Source: *Moundsville Weekly Echo*, July 20, 1906

W.G. Maxwell land

JULY 21

Faithful service

Rev. H.C. Sanford had been the chaplain for the penitentiary for five years. He was among the oldest Methodist ministers in West Virginia when he passed away on this day at the age of 83.
Source: *Moundsville Weekly Echo*, July 21, 1916

Rev. H. C. Sanford

JULY 22

Murderer dies

James Edward Jones murdered a young boy named Stanley Mason who lived in Moundsville. Jones died of tuberculosis and was buried in the prison cemetery.
Source: *Moundsville Weekly Echo*, July 22, 1898

Jacob Lutz executed in 1921

As Jacob Lutz was being taken to the Grafton jail by Chief of Police James Phillips, he pulled a revolver from his pocket. Lutz fired at Chief Phillips and missed wildly, but his second shot fatally wounded Phillips. Lutz was hanged and his funeral service was held at St. Francis Xavier Catholic Church in Moundsville.
Source: *"Pronounced Dead"* by C.J. Plogger

Jacob Lutz

JULY 23

Old inmate

John Adkins was convicted of breaking and entering a home and sent to the penitentiary. He was 76 years old.
Source: *Moundsville Daily Echo*, July 23, 1936

Another older inmate, Henry Kincaid, 95-years-old

Too much excitement

Because inmates became too animated the penitentiary staff decided to cut back on the number of R-rated movies shown at the prison.
Source: *Moundsville Daily Echo*, July 23, 1979

JULY 24

West Virginia's first serial killer

It was reported in the newspaper this day that Frank Johnson had confessed to murdering five people. He originally had denied it, but as his execution drew near, he wanted to clear his conscience.

Source: *Moundsville Weekly Echo*, July 24, 1908

Frank Johnson's mugshot

JULY 25

Making things right

Before Richard Collins was executed in 1946, he was
baptized in his cell on this date.
Source: *Moundsville Daily Echo*, July 25, 1946

Great author

Davis Grubb wrote two novels, *"Fool's Parade"* and the
"Night of the Hunter," loosely based on inmates at the
penitentiary. Grubb was a Moundsville native who later
moved to New York City.
Source: *Moundsville Daily Echo*, July 25, 1980

Davis Grubb

JULY 26

Hounds borrowed

The penitentiary bloodhounds were loaned to help find an 11-year-old deaf boy who was lost in a forest.
Source: *Moundsville Daily Echo*, July 26, 1954

Forest near the penitentiary

Saw his chance

Inmate James McGee was the prison sports reporter and traveled with the sports teams of the penitentiary when they went to games outside prison walls. McGee decided he had endured enough and successfully escaped during one of the outside games.
Source: *Moundsville Daily Echo*, July 26, 1958

JULY 27

A lot of food

During a weekend, inmates ate 592 pounds of pork, 55 pounds of bacon, 804 pounds of beef, 123 pounds of sugar, 130 pounds of rice, and 24 bushels of potatoes. They washed it down with 50 pounds of coffee.
Source: *Moundsville Weekly Echo*, July 27, 1906

Dining Hall where inmates ate

JULY 28

How many acres could 150 inmates farm?

Gov. William E. Glasscock wanted the prison Board of Control to find more land to farm for use by the penitentiary. He ordered the members to look for an area that could utilize the labor of 150 inmates.
Source: *Moundsville Journal*, July 28, 1910

Gov. William E. Glasscock

JULY 29

Checked out

An older inmate named Postlewaite escaped from the penitentiary when he went outside the walls to feed the hogs.
Source: *Moundsville Weekly Echo*, July 29, 1898

Carrying a gun

Correctional officers who were supervising inmates in the Brick Yard were allowed to carry guns.
Source: *Moundsville Weekly Echo*, July 29, 1898

Expanding

The penitentiary bought more land to the south so that it could expand and add more cells.
Source: *Moundsville Weekly Echo*, July 29, 1927

West Virginia Penitentiary

JULY 30

Prison mine

The prison mine was opened for inmates to start working in it. Prison officials projected that the mine would produce 3,400 tons of coal per acre.
Source: *Moundsville Weekly Echo*, July 30, 1920

Basement area where coal was kept

JULY 31

Clyde

Clyde was a bloodhound who chased inmates when they escaped from the penitentiary.
Source: *Moundsville Daily Echo*, July 31, 1973

Headline from *Moundsville Daily Echo*

AUGUST 1

Youngest life-termer

In September 1909, Charles Cook, 17, murdered 16-year-old Charles Bennett at the State Fairgrounds on Wheeling Island and threw his body from a bridge into the Ohio River. Cook received a life sentence and was the youngest life-termer in the pen. He did not have to serve his full sentence because he was pardoned at the age of 31

Source: *Moundsville Weekly Echo*, Aug. 1, 1919

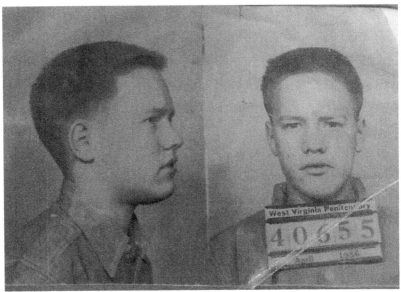

Mugshot of another young inmate, Tommy Williams,14, convicted of murder. Tommy spent 12 years in the penitentiary.

AUGUST 2

Giant inmate

An inmate from southern West Virginia was 6 feet, 6 inches tall and weighed 305 pounds. It was reported that he was the strongest man in the state of West Virginia.
Source: *Moundsville Weekly Echo*, Aug. 2, 1901

New cells in North Hall

The penitentiary added new cells to the North Hall. The work was done by inmates to save the expense of hiring laborers.
Source: *Moundsville Daily Echo*, Aug. 2, 1907

A more recent view of North Hall

AUGUST 3

Hot box

It was 96 degrees inside the cells in the penitentiary.
Source: *Moundsville Weekly Echo*, Aug. 3, 1917

Air conditioning in new dining hall

AUGUST 4

William Sutton executed in 1916

William Sutton murdered a doctor who was making a house call to see Sutton's brother. Sutton's motive for the killing was to cover up the robbery of Dr. J.J. Kennedy. Sutton was 19 when he committed the crime.
Source: *"Pronounced Dead"* by C.J. Plogger

William Sutton

Trying to alleviate overcrowding

Land was bought near Huttonsville to build another prison to help with penitentiary overcrowding problems. Huttonsville Correctional Center opened in 1939.
Source: *Moundsville Daily Echo*, Aug. 4, 1938

AUGUST 5

Not overcrowded yet

In 1892, there were 343 inmates incarcerated at the West Virginia Penitentiary.
Source: *Moundsville Weekly Echo*, Aug. 5, 1892

Hobart Grimm executed in 1921

Hobart Grimm was convicted of murdering Stephen Gelchek. Grimm adamantly denied he was the killer and instead named Mike Ondsick as the killer. Grimm admitted he helped Ondsick throw Gelchek's lifeless body from a bridge into the Ohio River, but maintained he was not the killer. Grimm was hanged and pronounced dead at 5:30 p.m.
Source: *"Pronounced Dead"* by C.J. Plogger

Hobart Grimm

AUGUST 6

Hugh Ferguson executed in 1919

Hugh Ferguson was only 23, but had served two prison terms in the penitentiary before he was sentenced to death. On April 7, 1919, he beat and raped Lola Zimmerman. He was hanged and pronounced dead at 5:34 p.m.
Source: *"Pronounced Dead"* by C.J. Plogger

Hugh Ferguson

AUGUST 7

Young convict

A 14-year-old boy was convicted of theft and sent to serve his sentence in the penitentiary.
Source: *Moundsville Weekly Echo*, Aug. 7, 1903

Former chaplain

F.W. Sigler became the parole and probation officer for the penitentiary in 1939. He had previously served as chaplain at the prison.
Source: *Moundsville Daily Echo*, Aug. 7, 1939

Penitentiary staff

AUGUST 8

Doctor fired

Dr. Joseph Peck was told by Warden M.L. Brown that his services were no longer required and he was fired from his position as the physician for the penitentiary.
Source: *Moundsville Weekly Echo*, Aug. 8, 1913

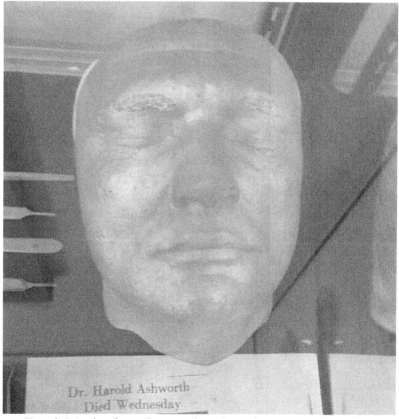

Dr. Harold Ashworth
Died Wednesday

Death Mask of another penitentiary doctor, Harold Ashworth

AUGUST 9

No more

Twelve inmates working in the shirt factory in the penitentiary refused to work any longer and went on strike at noon.
Source: *Moundsville Weekly Echo*, Aug. 9, 1918

West Virginia Penitentiary factory

AUGUST 10

Lawrence Fike executed in 1928

Lawrence Fike grabbed a heavy piece of wood and clubbed Elroy Leonard to death as Leonard was milking a cow. Fike then rummaged through Leonard's pockets and took his money. Fike was hanged and pronounced dead at 9:09 p.m.

Source: *"Pronounced Dead"* by C.J. Plogger

Lawrence Fike

Omer Brill executed in 1933

Omer Brill was 21 when he killed Lydia Burch and her 17-year-old daughter, Beatrice. Brill wanted to rob them, but only found 66 cents. He was hanged and pronounced dead at 9:14 p.m.

Source: *"Pronounced Dead"* by C.J. Plogger

Omer Brill

AUGUST 11

Joe Corey's final reprieve

Joe Corey and his wife, Ada, did not have a healthy marriage. After Ada requested a divorce, Corey walked into her workplace and shot Ada's cousin, Katherine Ghiz, and Ada, killing both of them. Corey received several reprieves because there was a concern that he was mentally impaired. Corey's final reprieve was on this date in 1933. He was eventually hanged for the double murder.

Source: *"Pronounced Dead"* by C.J. Plogger

Joe Corey

AUGUST 12

New truck

The penitentiary purchased a new truck that was 12 feet long and had a 6-foot-wide bed. On the sides of the truck, the name of the penitentiary was printed in gold letters. Source: *Moundsville Weekly Echo*, Aug. 12, 1915

West Virginia Penitentiary truck

AUGUST 13

Close call

While Tom Walker was delivering supplies to the prison with a horse and wagon through the North Wagon Gate entrance, the hinges of an inside gate pulled loose from the wall. The heavy gate fell on the wagon smashing it and barely missing Walker and his horse.
Source: *Moundsville Weekly Echo*, Aug. 13, 1897

Moved to death cell

Phillip Euman was the youngest inmate to be executed. On this date, he was moved to the death cell so that the death penalty could be exacted.
Source: *"Pronounced Dead"* by C.J. Plogger

Phillip Euman

AUGUST 14

Attempted suicide

Correctional Officer W.G. Brown attempted to commit suicide because he was distraught after witnessing an execution at the penitentiary. The gun slipped from his hands before he could pull the trigger.
Source: *Moundsville Weekly Echo*, Aug. 14, 1903

Noose used for an execution

AUGUST 15

Barber fight

The barbers union of Moundsville petitioned the penitentiary to stop the inmates from cutting hair because the barbers were losing business. The vote at the penitentiary was a tie so it was decided that only members of the barbers union could shave clients.
Source: *Moundsville Weekly Echo*, Aug. 15, 1902

Former area of barber shop

AUGUST 16

Young inmate

A young Hispanic boy was released from the penitentiary
after serving 10 years. Ten years earlier, he got into a
fight in Fairmont and shot three men. There is no record
of his age, only that he was a small boy.
Source: *Moundsville Weekly Echo*, Aug. 16, 1907

Fairmont, West Virginia

AUGUST 17

Outnumbered

In 1894 there were 458 inmates being supervised by 15 correctional officers working on the day shift and five correctional officers working the night shift.
Source: *Moundsville Weekly Echo*, Aug. 17, 1894

West Virginia Penitentiary Correctional Officer

AUGUST 18

Klee's factory

The Klee's Clothing factory inside the prison employed 450 employees and paid the penitentiary 25 cents a day each for their labor.
Source: *Moundsville Weekly Echo*, Aug. 18, 1905

Many inmates

In 1926, there were 2,500 inmates in a prison designed to hold only 800.
Source: *Moundsville Daily Echo*, Aug. 18, 1926

K Block of New Wall

AUGUST 19

Open for labor

The prison mine was in full operation and the inmates working in it could earn up to seven-and-a-half good days for their labor.
Source: *Moundsville Weekly Echo*, Aug. 19, 1921

Area formerly occupied by the prison mine

AUGUST 20

Philip Euman executed in 1926

Philip Euman, 18, was the youngest inmate executed at the penitentiary. He murdered 19-year-old Charles Shaw, who was a grocery clerk. There was a great deal of effort exerted to commute Euman's sentence to life in prison because he was so young. All of the work was unsuccessful. He was hanged and pronounced dead at 5:11 p.m.
Source: *"Pronounced Dead"* by C.J. Plogger

Philip Euman

AUGUST 21

Buried in South Yard

Inmate George Hickman died after a lingering illness and was buried in what is now the South Yard of the prison. Inmates buried there were moved the next year, 1897, to the prison cemetery named White Gate Cemetery.
Source: *Moundsville Weekly Echo*, Aug. 21, 1896

White Gate Cemetery

AUGUST 22

Unsubstantiated rumor

A rumor flew through town that 30 inmates had escaped from the prison one night.
Source: *Moundsville Weekly Echo*, Aug. 22, 1902

Too many

The penitentiary had room for only 900 inmates but housed 2,106.
Source: *Moundsville Daily Echo*, Aug. 22, 1940

Not a wise choice

Vivian Crow was arrested after bringing alcohol into the penitentiary for the inmates.
Source: *Moundsville Daily Echo*, Aug. 22, 1959

Headline from *Moundsville Daily Echo*

AUGUST 23

Improving themselves

In 1955, 35 inmates learned to read and write.
Source: *Moundsville Daily Echo*, Aug. 23, 1955

Classroom in penitentiary

Long break

Inmate Bruce Skaggs escaped from the penitentiary in
1925, but was not recaptured until 1956.
Source: *Moundsville Daily Echo*, Aug. 23, 1956

AUGUST 24

A lot of miles

Correctional Officer A.J. Coleman traveled 6,000 miles in one month to bring inmates to the penitentiary. His longest trip was to San Antonio, Texas, to pick up Alfred Maynard, who had murdered his wife.
Source: *Moundsville Daily Echo*, Aug. 24, 1915

San Antonio, Texas

AUGUST 25

Not a good end

Burrel Forgey was sentenced to life in prison on murder and armed robbery convictions. Overwhelmed, he committed suicide by drinking chloroform.
Source: *Moundsville Journal*, Aug. 25, 1910

AUGUST 26

Many guests

In 1904, there were 1,067 inmates in the penitentiary.
Source: *Moundsville Weekly Echo*, Aug. 26, 1904

West Virginia Penitentiary

Not out long

Inmate James Thomas escaped from the prison farm and
was later captured in Mineral County.
Source: *Moundsville Daily Echo*, Aug. 26, 1907

AUGUST 27

Arthur Brown executed in 1909

Arthur Brown murdered an 18-year-old boy, Robert Shannon, after he robbed him of the grocery money his mother gave him to buy food for the family. Brown was hanged and pronounced dead at 5:06 p.m.
Source: *"Pronounced Dead"* by C.J. Plogger

Arthur Brown

Ladies leaving

The female inmates left the penitentiary to be housed at the Lakin Correctional Center in Mason County in 1947.
Source: West Virginia Penitentiary Museum *"Notebook No. 3"*

AUGUST 28

Spent time well

An inmate released after serving three years in the penitentiary used his prison time wisely. He took a course in machinery by correspondence from a school in Chicago and received his diploma and degree when he left.
Source: *Moundsville Weekly Echo*, Aug. 28, 1908

Regretting his action

Albert William murdered his wife by stabbing her with a pair of scissors during a drunken argument. When he was locked up, he repeatedly beat his head against the bars and pleaded not to be hanged. He was sentenced to life in prison and was not executed.
Source: *Moundsville Weekly Echo*, Aug. 28, 1908

Cell bars

AUGUST 29

Close call

While Correctional Officer Frank Burgy was walking the walls by Tower No. 3, he was shot at with a .32-caliber bullet. The bullet struck the wall two inches below his foot, but did not harm him.
Source: *Moundsville Weekly Echo*, Aug. 29, 1904

Tower No. 3

Union
In 1984, West Virginia Penitentiary correctional officers tried to organize a union to protect their rights.
Source: *Moundsville Daily Echo*, Aug. 29, 1984

AUGUST 30

Helping the town

In 1907, the inmates paved 10th Street in Moundsville to provide better transportation for the townspeople.
Source: *Moundsville Weekly Echo*, Aug. 30, 1907

Road paved by inmates

AUGUST 31

Not sticking around

Inmates Melvin Miller and Charles Kilgore escaped from the prison farm.
Source: *Moundsville Daily Echo*, Aug. 31, 1943

Prison farm correctional officers
Correctional Officer Gerald Ebert, far left
Captain William Wallace, far right.
Three center officers are unidentified.

SEPTEMBER 1

James Lay executed in 1916

James Lay murdered William Bowman as he was robbing him. No one worked on behalf of Lay for a reprieve and he was hanged without friends or family present.
Source: *"Pronounced Dead"* by C.J. Plogger

JAMES LAY   #9681

McDowell County

Executed   Sept. 1, 1916

James Lay

SEPTEMBER 2

Visitors

A group of teachers visited the penitentiary at the invitation of Warden Charles E. Haddox.
Source: *Moundsville Weekly Echo*, Sept. 2, 1904

Headstone of Warden Charles E. Haddox

SEPTEMBER 3

Too many inmates

There were 1,994 inmates in the penitentiary.
Source: *Moundsville Weekly Echo*, Sept. 3, 1926

Solitary confinement

Three inmates, Waverly Childern, Pete Ferguson, and
Jim Williams, were placed in solitary confinement
because they stabbed correctional officers while they
were working in the shirt factory.
Source: *Moundsville Weekly Echo*, Sept. 3, 1926

One of the "Holes" used for solitary confinement

SEPTEMBER 4

Examined for lunacy

Two inmates were being examined because of bizarre behavior and faced charges of lunacy.
Source: *Moundsville Weekly Echo*, Sept. 4, 1903

Cell in Special Programs Unit or "psych ward"

Being generous

The penitentiary gave 15,000 tons of coal mined from the prison mine to needy families.
Source: *Moundsville Daily Echo*, Sept. 4, 1934

Crash landing

Capt. Coffee crash landed on the prison farm as he was flying to a close friend's funeral. The plane ran out of gas and stopped short of his Pennsylvania destination.
Source: *Moundsville Daily Echo*, Sept. 4, 1943

SEPTEMBER 5

Moved to Moundsville

Five inmates from the Huttonsville Correctional Center
were moved to the penitentiary in Moundsville because
they started a riot in Huttonsville.
Source: *Moundsville Daily Echo*, Sept. 5, 1978

Huttonsville Correctional Center

SEPTEMBER 6

Old horse thief

A 70-year-old man from Preston County was taken to the penitentiary because he was a chronic horse thief.
Source: *Moundsville Weekly Echo*, Sept. 6, 1912

Multiple murders

Five bodies were found buried at Harry Power's farm in Quiet Dell. He was later convicted of two murders and executed at the penitentiary.
Source: *Moundsville Daily Echo*, Sept. 6, 1932

Harry Powers

SEPTEMBER 7

Robert Hopkins executed in 1956

Robert Hopkins murdered a car dealer named Thomas Ervine. Hopkins was electrocuted on "Old Sparky" and pronounced dead at 9:12 p.m.
Source: *"Pronounced Dead"* by C.J. Plogger

HOPKINS, Robert Lee #40669

Robert Hopkins

SEPTEMBER 8

Loyal family

A man from Wayne County was sentenced to the penitentiary. His wife and young daughter followed him and lived in Moundsville until he served his time.
Source: *Moundsville Weekly Echo*, Sept. 8, 1905

Smuggling in booze

National Bed Co. foreman Edward Allison was arrested at the penitentiary because he was smuggling alcohol to inmates. An inmate named Robert Rucker turned him in after he was caught with the liquor.
Source: *Moundsville Weekly Echo*, Sept. 8, 1911

National Bed Co. factory was later converted to a hospital

SEPTEMBER 9

George Williams executed in 1904

George Williams assaulted a 20-year-old teacher named
Laura Knade. He was hanged and pronounced dead at
5:29 p.m.
Source: *"Pronounced Dead"* by C.J. Plogger

George Williams

SEPTEMBER 10

Charles Forrest executed in 1915

Charles Forrest and Will Hyden were selling moonshine together and got into a heated argument. In the midst of their passionate discourse, Forrest stabbed Hyden to death. Forrest was hanged and pronounced dead at 5:23 p.m.
Source: *"Pronounced Dead"* by C.J. Plogger

Henry Jackson executed in 1926

Henry Jackson was confronted by Correctional Officer Earl Langfitt in the Dining Hall for breaking the rules. Jackson, who had been incarcerated before because of violence, plunged a dagger into Officer Langfitt's neck killing him. Langfitt was the first officer to die in the line of duty in the penitentiary. Jackson was hanged and pronounced dead at 5:13 p.m.
Source: *"Pronounced Dead"* by C.J. Plogger

Mervin Brown executed in 1937

Mervin Brown smashed 85-year-old James Garland over the head with an iron pipe because he wanted to rob him of an insurance policy that was worth $150. James died as a result of the blow. Brown was hanged and pronounced dead at 9:03 p.m.
Source: *"Pronounced Dead"* by C.J. Plogger

Charles Forrest Henry Jackson Mervin Brown

SEPTEMBER 11

New cells

Construction of 180 new cells was completed in the North Hall and the building for women was ready for occupancy two weeks later.
Source: *Moundsville Weekly Echo*, Sept. 11, 1903

North Hall

SEPTEMBER 12

Tiny McCoy executed in 1924

Tiny McCoy and his 22-year-old wife, Hallie, did not get along well and after a terrible argument, Hallie fled to the home of her parents. Enraged, McCoy followed her and then murdered Hallie, his mother-in-law, Mary Totten, and his brother-in-law, William Totten. McCoy was hanged and pronounced dead at 5:07 p.m.
Source: *"Pronounced Dead"* by C.J. Plogger

Tiny McCoy

SEPTEMBER 13

First woman almost hanged

Matilene Dean shot and killed Mack Nixon, nicknamed Shamrock, who had been following and harassing her. She was sentenced to be hanged, but appealed and the sentence was reversed because of claims of racial discrimination since she was an African-American. There were no women executed at the West Virginia Penitentiary.
Source: *State vs. Dean, 58, S.E. 2d 860, 1950, Supreme Court of Appeals of West Virginia*

Millard Morrison and Walter Wilmot executed in 1929

Millard Morrison and Walter Wilmot murdered gas station owner Frank Bowen. During their trials, both men accused the other of committing the crime. They were hanged at the same time and both were pronounced dead at 8:51 p.m.
Source: *"Pronounced Dead"* by C.J. Plogger

Millard Morrison   Walter Wilmot

SEPTEMBER 14

Young escapee

Charles Slone, 18, escaped while he was working on a road crew.
Source: *Moundsville Daily Echo*, Sept. 14, 1943

West Virginia inmate road crew

SEPTEMBER 15

Tired of making bread

Russell Mounts was sentenced to five to 18 years in the penitentiary for murder. He escaped because he said he was tired of staying up late making the bread for the other inmates. He knew that after 9 p.m. there would be no correctional officers in the towers so he successfully scaled the walls and escaped.
Source: *Moundsville Weekly Echo*, Sept. 15, 1922

West Virginia Penitentiary Tower No. 1

SEPTEMBER 16

Baby girl

In 1904, 18-year-old inmate Charlotte Hawkins was serving a seven-year sentence in the penitentiary for larceny. She delivered a healthy baby girl in the evening.
Source: *Moundsville Weekly Echo*, Sept. 16, 1904

Struck by lightning

On a blustery Tuesday at 6:30 a.m., the flagpole on top of the main administration building of the penitentiary was struck by lightning and torn to splinters.
Source: *Moundsville Weekly Echo*, Sept. 16, 1910

West Virginia Penitentiary

SEPTEMBER 17

Warden baffled by escapes

In the space of a month, five inmates escaped from the penitentiary and Warden J.Z. Terrell was baffled. He remarked, "I hate to charge these escapes to carelessness on the part of the guards and am more inclined to believe that there is some mysterious influence working on the prisoners or it may be a runaway spell."
Source: *Moundsville Weekly Echo*, Sept. 17, 1920

JOSEPH Z. TERRELL.
Warden J.Z. Terrell

SEPTEMBER 18

Starting to boom

In 1894, there were 430 inmates in the penitentiary.
Source: *Moundsville Weekly Echo*, Sept. 18, 1894

New cells with toilets

The South Hall cells were replaced and the new ones had "lavatories" or toilets. The West Virginia Penitentiary was one of the first prisons in the United States to have running water in the cells.
Source: *Moundsville Weekly Echo*, Sept. 18, 1918

South Hall cells

SEPTEMBER 19

Poetic murderer

A few hours before Tiny McCoy was executed on Sept. 12, 1924, for multiple murders, he wrote a poem. The poem was widely disseminated and many people read it. The poem, "Dear friends, you're truly welcome to be with us today, and we hope you will sit quiet while we shall sing and pray. Hope you'll listen quietly to every word that is said, and when you leave this place, you'll say how richly we were fed."
Source: *Moundsville Weekly Echo*, Sept. 19, 1924

Tiny McCoy

SEPTEMBER 20

Presidential candidate

Eugene Debs served time in the penitentiary and was transferred to the Atlanta Federal Penitentiary. While there, he ran for president of the United States and received 919,799 votes.
Source: *Moundsville Weekly Echo*, Sept. 20, 1918

EUGENE V. DEBS.

Eugene Debs

Prison mine

The prison mine was nearly ready to open on this date. It had been dug to a depth of 20 feet.
Source: *Moundsville Weekly Echo*, Sept. 20, 1920

SEPTEMBER 21

Ingenious escape attempt

Inmate Frank Hayden hid inside a box of dry goods that was going to be shipped out of the penitentiary. Hayden got as far as the train station before he was discovered and was returned to the penitentiary.
Source: *Moundsville Weekly Echo*, Sept. 21, 1917

Moundsville train station

Inmate wrestlers

Little Beaver, Earthquake, and Little Hog Head were the names of some of the inmates who wrestled in the penitentiary. The events were open to the public and provided fascinating entertainment.
Source: *Moundsville Daily Echo*, Sept. 21, 1962

SEPTEMBER 22

Attractive female inmate

Mrs. Blackshire was convicted as an accomplice to the murder of her husband and was sentenced to three years in the penitentiary. When she arrived at the train station there was a crowd waiting to see her. She was described as "handsome."
Source: *Moundsville Weekly Echo*, Sept. 22, 1905

Different look

In 1971, the older buildings in the North Yard of the penitentiary were torn down because of safety and security concerns.
Source: *Moundsville Daily Echo*, Sept. 22, 1971

North Yard of the penitentiary

SEPTEMBER 23

Matthew Perison executed in 1948

Matthew Perison was a coal miner who was unhappily married to his wife, Clancy. During a heated argument, he chopped her to death with an ax. His anger did not subside so he found Clancy's parents, Jack and Pearl Martin, and murdered them. He was hanged and became the only inmate hanged on a Thursday.
Source: *"Pronounced Dead"* by C.J. Plogger

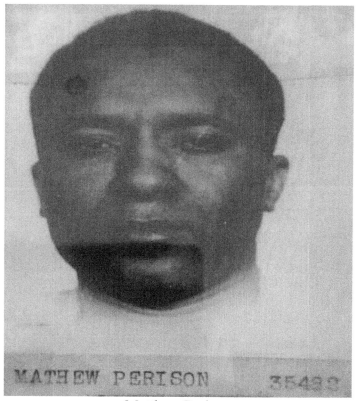

Matthew Perison

SEPTEMBER 24

Could not stop loving

William Watkins was in love with Fannie Hildebrand, but was heartbroken when she married someone else. Unable to move on, Watkins murdered Fannie and was sentenced to life imprisonment in the penitentiary.
Source: *Moundsville Weekly Echo*, Sept. 24, 1915

Cemetery where Fannie Hildebrand is buried

SEPTEMBER 25

Stabbed in the kitchen

In 1903, an inmate was stabbed in the kitchen on Sunday morning. He was still alive at 2 p.m., but was not expected to survive.
Source: *Moundsville Weekly Echo*, Sept. 25, 1903

Freezer in the penitentiary kitchen

Almost got away

Inmate Fred Facemeyer escaped from the penitentiary in a box being transported by a wagon. When the wagon reached Third Street, Facemeyer jumped out of the box and Correctional Officer Joseph Rinehart saw him, recognized him, and chased him until he caught him a few blocks away.
Source: *Moundsville Weekly Echo*, Sept. 25, 1925

SEPTEMBER 26

Moonshining

Eli Barson was fined $300 and sentenced to three years in the penitentiary for possessing moonshine and a still.
Source: *Moundsville Weekly Echo*, Sept. 26, 1924

Seized the opportunity

In 1964, a fuse blew at the North Wagon Gate shutting down its power. Three inmates took advantage of the situation by escaping through the open door.
Source: *Moundsville Daily Echo,* Sept. 26, 1964

North Wagon Gate

SEPTEMBER 27

High percentage incarcerated

In 1895, 33 percent of the population of the penitentiary was African-American inmates while the African-American population in West Virginia was only 4 percent.

Source: *Moundsville Weekly Echo*, Sept. 27, 1895

Mural of state seal painted on penitentiary wall

SEPTEMBER 28

A lot of tomatoes

In 1894, inmates ate 14 bushels of tomatoes each meal.
Source: *Moundsville Weekly Echo*, Sept. 28, 1894

Inmates' health improving

The health of the inmates improved because they had
pure water after new wells were drilled in the North
Yard.
Source: *Moundsville Weekly Echo*, Sept. 28, 1894

Water towers in penitentiary

SEPTEMBER 29

Tired of being out

Inmate Walter Mays escaped from the penitentiary in 1942, but decided he wanted to return. A year later, he walked back to the penitentiary and turned himself in.
Source: *Moundsville Daily Echo*, Sept. 29, 1942

Well-known inmate escaped

Well-known inmate William "Red" Snyder escaped from the penitentiary by hiding underneath a pile of bricks stacked on the garbage truck.
Source: *Moundsville Daily Echo*, Sept. 29, 1972

William "Red" Snyder

SEPTEMBER 30

Typhoid fever

Inmate W.S. Douglass was serving a life sentence in the penitentiary for murder, but many people believed he was innocent. He died of typhoid fever.
Source: *Moundsville Weekly Echo*, Sept. 30, 1892

Burial service at White Gate Cemetery

OCTOBER 1

Moonshining Momma

Katie Kolinski went to trial for moonshining and was found guilty. She was sentenced to serve three years. The case was unusual because most entrepreneurial moonshiners were male.
Source: *Moundsville Weekly Echo*, Oct. 1, 1926

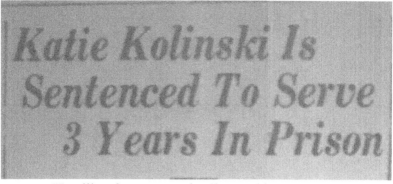

Headline from *Moundsville Weekly Echo*

OCTOBER 2

Sad situation

Penitentiary clerk John Laughlin was in a great deal of pain from injuries he suffered in an explosion in which he lost his leg. He later shot himself after leaving a farewell letter to his wife stating he was tired of life. He was 50 years old and had two children.
Source: *Moundsville Weekly Echo*, Oct. 2, 1903

Clever hiding spot

In 1908, an inmate hid in the pump organ in the chapel hoping to find an opportunity to escape.
Source: M*oundsville Weekly Echo*, Oct. 2, 1908

Pump organ at the penitentiary

Female federal prisoners

Female federal prisoners were transferred from the Tennessee State Penitentiary to Moundsville because there was not enough room for them in federal penitentiaries.
Source: *Moundsville Weekly Echo*, Oct. 2, 1908

OCTOBER 3

Forgot where he was standing

Correctional Officers Church Marsh and H.F. Williams were standing on a 40-foot high trestle of the B&O Railroad looking for an escaped convict named Alexander Childs. About 3 p.m., Marsh saw a man resembling Childs running down 7th Street. Eager to get a closer look, Marsh accidentally stepped off the side of the trestle. He fell to the ground, was knocked unconscious from the fall, and his head was badly cut.
Source: *Moundsville Weekly Echo*, Oct. 3, 1913

7th street in Moundsville
Note the penitentiary in the background.

Left but returned

Inmate Michael Miller was paroled, but quickly rearrested and returned to the penitentiary because he was convicted of killing an inmate named James Hall when Miller was serving time.
Source: Moundsville Daily Echo, Oct. 3, 1985

OCTOBER 4

Big send off

Warden M.Z. White served the penitentiary for four years
from 1914 to 1918 and retired with an elaborate party.
His initials stand for Montezuma.
Source: *Moundsville Weekly Echo*, Oct. 4, 1918

M. Z. WHITE
WARDEN PENITENTIARY

OCTOBER 5

Correctional officer made ultimate sacrifice

Correctional Officer William Quilliams was murdered in the penitentiary by inmate Bobby Gene Jarvis.
Source: *Moundsville Daily Echo*, Oct. 5, 1972

Correctional Officer William Quilliams

OCTOBER 6

Fire

A fire raged in the National Bed Plant in the penitentiary at 10:30 p.m. on a Saturday night. Warden M.L. Brown reported that it probably was not intentional but carelessness in handling waste materials located in the plant. The damage was estimated at $200 to $300.
Source: *Moundsville Weekly Echo*, Oct. 6, 1911

Headline from *The Wheeling Register*

OCTOBER 7

Henry Harbor executed in 1921

Henry Harbor became entangled in a vicious argument
with his wife, Mildred Robinson. Unable to contain his
anger he killed her with a butcher knife. He was hanged
and pronounced dead at 5:40 p.m.
Source: *"Pronounced Dead"* by C.J. Plogger

Henry Harbor

OCTOBER 8

Long sentence

Roy Conkle was given the moniker "King of Moundsville bootleggers" and sent to the penitentiary for six years. His was among the harshest and longest sentences to be handed down for a liquor law conviction. Source: *Moundsville Weekly Echo*, Oct. 8, 1926

Moundsville, West Virginia

OCTOBER 9

Population growing

In 1896 there were 581 inmates in the penitentiary.
Source: *Moundsville Weekly Echo*, Oct. 9, 1896

Unusual transport team

Sheriff Hatfield and six deputies brought 10 inmates to
the penitentiary. They were accompanied by their wives
because they wanted to spend the night in "musical"
Wheeling. A question was raised if the wives should
have received a per diem and mileage allowance.
Source: *Moundsville Weekly Echo*, Oct. 9, 1903

Capital Theater in Wheeling

OCTOBER 10

Shep Caldwell executed in 1899

Shep Caldwell was the first man to be executed at the penitentiary. He had murdered his mistress, Rose Crenshaw, after finding her with another man. He was hanged at 1a.m. on a Tuesday morning and pronounced dead 10 minutes later.

Source: *"Pronounced Dead"* by C.J. Plogger

Shep Caldwell

OCTOBER 11

Richard Lee Collins executed in 1946

Richard Collins normally did not bother anyone, but he tried to steal a car from a used car dealer named Denver Hill. Hill resisted him and Collins drew a handgun and shot him to death. He was hanged and pronounced dead at 8:58 p.m.

Source: *"Pronounced Dead"* by C.J. Plogger

Richard Collins

OCTOBER 12

Visitors charged

Visitors paid 25 cents to visit penitentiary inmates.
Source: *Moundsville Weekly Echo*, Oct. 12, 1894.

Sign leading to non-contact visiting area

Stone cells replaced

In 1906, the original stone cells in the South Hall of the
penitentiary were replaced by steel cells.
Source: *Moundsville Weekly Echo*, Oct. 12, 1906

OCTOBER 13

Not welcome here

Warden J.Z. Terrell told inmates released from the penitentiary that they could not stay or reside in Moundsville.
Source: *Moundsville Weekly Echo*, Oct. 13, 1922

Moundsville, West Virginia

OCTOBER 14

Low pay

In 1898, a correctional officer at the penitentiary made $60 a month.
Source: *Moundsville Weekly Echo*, Oct. 14, 1898

Honor guard of West Virginia Division of Corrections

OCTOBER 15

Lemuel Steed executed in 1948

Lemuel Steed wanted to rob Dr. Loren McClung of his employee payroll of $8,000, but went farther and shot him to death. In a locker rented by Steed, $6,000 was found later. He was hanged and pronounced dead at 9:15 p.m.
Source: *"Pronounced Dead"* by C.J. Plogger

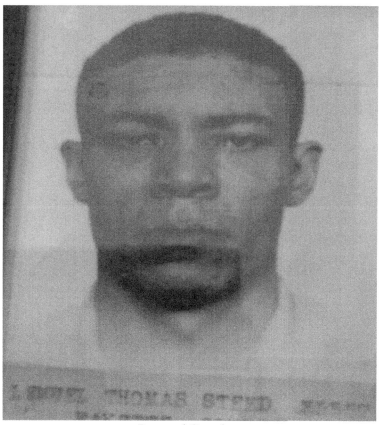
Lemuel Steed

OCTOBER 16

Glove factory

The A.T. Halloch Co., which manufactured gloves and mittens, leased space in the penitentiary for three years and 100 inmates were employed there.
Source: *Moundsville Weekly Echo*, Oct. 16, 1896

Volstead Act

The Volstead Act passed in 1919 prohibited the transportation, manufacturing, importing or sales of alcoholic beverages. Don Chafin would serve a two-year sentence at the penitentiary as he was convicted of violating the Volstead Act at the federal courthouse in Huntington on Oct. 14, 1924. Chafin appealed and the verdict was upheld in a ruling in April 1925. He was sheriff of Logan County from 1912 to 1924, immediately prior to his moonshining conviction. While sheriff, he was a fierce opponent of unionization and received hundreds of thousands of dollars from coal mine operators in return for his violent suppression of the United Mine Workers union.
Source: *Moundsville Weekly Echo*, Oct. 16, 1925

Prohibition headlines

OCTOBER 17

Not a successful escape

Paul McCracken and Earl Blankenship tried to escape from the penitentiary by strong-arming correctional officers. They then hid in the Broom Factory where they later were going to scale the walls to escape. They were discovered, however, and were shot and later died of their wounds.

Source: *Moundsville Weekly Echo*, Oct. 17, 1907

Broom Factory in penitentiary

OCTOBER 18

A lot of bricks

In 1892, the penitentiary sold 20,000 of the lighter salmon-colored bricks that were manufactured there. Source: *Moundsville Weekly Echo*, Oct. 18, 1892

Bricks made at the penitentiary

OCTOBER 19

18-hour riot

In 1951, 1,800 inmates rioted at the penitentiary for 18 hours because they were angry about the quantity and quality of the food.
Source: *Moundsville Daily Echo*, Oct. 19, 1951

1973 Riot

OCTOBER 20

Back and forth

John Rentforth killed John Gorman in Parkersburg and was sent to the penitentiary. Because of his youth, he was then taken from the penitentiary to reform school, but Special Judge George Neal ruled that he should return to the penitentiary.
Source: *Moundsville Weekly Echo*, Oct. 20, 1905

Parkersburg, West Virginia

OCTOBER 21

Wheat theft

John Gatts and Charles Henthorn were convicted of stealing wheat from a granary and were sentenced to serve one year in the penitentiary.
Source: *Moundsville Weekly Echo*, Oct. 21, 1888

West Virginia Penitentiary

OCTOBER 22

Revenge

Oscar Pipps had a problem with another inmate, William Banks, and attacked him. Banks, being much stronger, simply pushed Pipps away, humiliating him. After a month in solitary confinement, Pipps exacted his revenge by stabbing and killing Banks with one blade of sharpened scissors.
Source: *Moundsville Weekly Echo*, Oct. 22, 1909

License plates

In 1977, inmates started stamping the West Virginia state tourism slogan on the license plates.
Source: *Moundsville Daily Echo*, Oct. 22, 1977

West Virginia Penitentiary Museum
Inmates added urine to the paint to give the plates a yellow tint.

OCTOBER 23

Prison farm successful

In 1908, the prison farm produced 5,489 dozen onions, 2,210 bushels of potatoes, 1,594 dozen cucumbers, and 7,536 gallons of milk.
Source: *Moundsville Weekly Echo*, Oct. 23, 1908

Prison farm

New magazine

Inmates started publishing a magazine that featured events occurring at the penitentiary. It was called *"Work and Hope."*
Source: *Moundsville Weekly Echo*, Oct. 23, 1919

OCTOBER 24

State Henry executed in 1902

State Henry was convicted of murdering John Richardson with a hammer, but there was some question of his guilt. A man who had been hanged in Uniontown, Pa., had confessed to murdering Richardson and even filled out 19 affidavits saying he was the perpetrator of the crime. Among Henry's last words were "they are going to kill an innocent man." He was hanged and pronounced dead at 5:49 p.m.

Source: *"Pronounced Dead"* by CJ. Plogger

State Henry

OCTOBER 25

Sick

At least seven cases of smallpox were discovered at the penitentiary.
Source: *Moundsville Weekly Echo*, Oct. 25, 1895

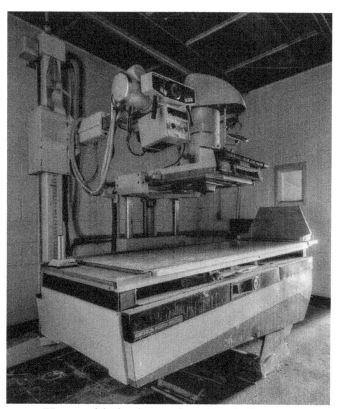

X-ray table in the penitentiary infirmary

Pardon for young inmate

Zack Hartwell received a life sentence, but was later given a pardon by Gov. Albert B. White because Hartwell was only 15 years old at the time of the crime.
Source: *Moundsville Weekly Echo*, Oct. 25, 1901

OCTOBER 26

Not many successful escapes

Warden C.F. McClintic reported that 90 percent of escapees in the last three years had been recaptured. Source: *Moundsville Daily Echo*, Oct. 26, 1936

Three inmates who escaped on Feb. 19, 1992

OCTOBER 27

Entrepreneurs

Four men, Dick Welcher, Gussie Williams, Elbert Nashburn, and Jack Brown, were sentenced to serve a year in the penitentiary for selling cocaine.
Source: *Moundsville Weekly Echo*, Oct. 27, 1911

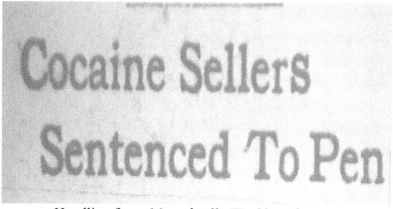

Headline from *Moundsville Weekly Echo*

OCTOBER 28

New lights

In 1899, a new lighting system was installed at the penitentiary because most of the earlier lighting involved burning coal.
Source: *Moundsville Weekly Echo*, Oct. 28, 1899

Breaker box by the "Wheel"

OCTOBER 29

Black Hand gang

The Black Hand gang was starting to reach into West Virginia. The gang was made up of Italian immigrants who used extortion and murder for illicit gain. Four Black Hand gang members were among the 94 executions at the penitentiary.

Source: *Moundsville Weekly Echo*, Oct. 29, 1915

Black Hand Gang

OCTOBER 30

Got away with it

Inmate George Hill stabbed and wounded inmate James Taylor. Hill was acquitted and avoided an additional sentence.
Source: *Moundsville Weekly Echo*, Oct. 30, 1908

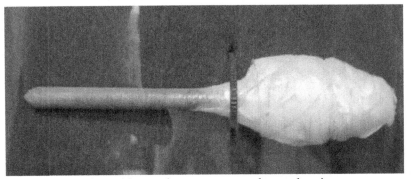

Weapon fashioned by an inmate to attack another inmate

OCTOBER 31

Riot!

Nine hundred inmates working at the Kleeson and Gordon factory rioted for four days, protesting a new work system and the food they received. They eventually calmed down with no loss of life.
Source: *Moundsville Weekly Echo*, Oct. 31, 1924

Kleeson and Gordon factory in penitentiary

NOVEMBER 1

Not a long sentence

In 1895, Frank Duncan received only a six-year sentence in the penitentiary after being convicted of second-degree murder.
Source: *Moundsville Weekly Echo*, Nov. 1, 1895

West Virginia Penitentiary

NOVEMBER 2

George Barrage executed in 1937

George Barrage had a deadly secret. He murdered a man in Pennsylvania, changed his name, and moved to West Virginia with his wife, Katherine. Paranoia set in and Barrage became concerned his wife would turn him in to the authorities, so he murdered her. He was hanged and pronounced dead at 5:27 p.m.
Source: *"Pronounced Dead"* by C.J. Plogger

George Barrage

NOVEMBER 3

First African-American staff woman

Annie Jones was the first African-American woman to
work in the penitentiary as an assistant matron
supervising female prisoners.
Source: *Moundsville Weekly Echo*, Nov. 3, 1918

Women's cell in the penitentiary

NOVEMBER 4

Special visitor

"Mother" Elizabeth Wheaton was a well-known prison evangelist who had traveled to every prison in the United States and ministered to inmates. On this date, she visited the Moundsville penitentiary.
Source: *Moundsville Weekly Echo*, Nov. 4, 1910

"Mother" Elizabeth Wheaton

Crafty plan

Inmate Rufus Beam tried to escape from the penitentiary by hiding in an outgoing box of shirts.
Source: *Moundsville Weekly Echo*, Nov. 4, 1921

NOVEMBER 5

William Read executed in 1923

William Read was a very troubled person. He and two others severely beat 68-year-old Ellwood Matthews and then Read shot him three times in the head. Later, Read beat another man, Earle Dollman, and threw his body under a burning car where he died. Read was hanged and pronounced dead at 9:03 p.m.
Source: *"Pronounced Dead"* by C.J. Plogger

William Read

NOVEMBER 6

Quite a racket

William Jenkins stole a yoke of oxen from a man and then sold them to another man. Later, Jenkins stole the oxen again and returned them to the rightful owner asking for a reward for finding them. His plot was discovered and he was sent to the penitentiary.
Source: *Moundsville Weekly Echo*, Nov. 6, 1891

Quick escape

Inmate Docker escaped from the penitentiary after a correctional officer challenged him to a foot race. The officer said if Docker could outrun him, he could keep going to freedom, and he did.
Source: *Moundsville Weekly Echo*, Nov. 6, 1903

Jefferson Avenue in front of the penitentiary

Many cells

In 1903, there were 841 cells in the penitentiary to house inmates. It would not be long before more cells would be needed to hold the prisoners.
Source: *Moundsville Weekly Echo*, Nov. 6, 1903

NOVEMBER 7

Worst escape

In 1979, 15 inmates, including; Ronald Turney Williams, Jack Hart, Donald Layne, Harold Gower, Jimmy Collins and others escaped through the front door of the penitentiary. They had taken two correctional officers, Jerry Daff and John Villers, hostage as they absconded. On the street, off-duty West Virginia State Trooper Philip Kesner's car was stopped and he and his wife were pulled from the vehicle. Trooper Kesner was able to shoot and kill one escaping inmate, Jimmy Collins, but Kesner was also shot and paid the ultimate sacrifice of his life.
Source: *"Pronounced Dead"* by C.J. Plogger

West Virginia State Trooper Philip Kesner

NOVEMBER 8

Lying

Three inmates, Jerry Jackson, Billy Moore, and Luther Dingess, were convicted of perjury for their claims that they were being mistreated at the penitentiary.
Source: *Moundsville Daily Echo*, Nov. 8, 1968

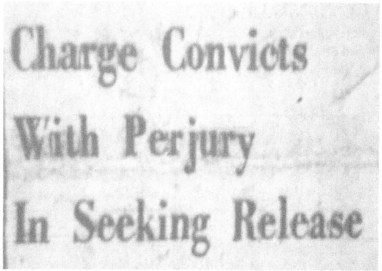

Headline from *Moundsville Daily Echo*

NOVEMBER 9

Frank Broadenax executed in 1899

At a railroad camp, Frank Broadenax had a rusty pistol that he believed could not be fired. He jokingly pointed it at 16-year-old Sherman McFadden, pulled the trigger and the gun discharged. Frank paid $50 to a doctor to try to save Sherman, but the youth died. Broadenax received one stay of execution, but later Gov. George W. Atkinson determined he had to be hanged. Broadenax was hanged and after his neck broke, his body twitched in agony for 14 minutes.
Source: *"Pronounced Dead"* by C.J. Plogger

Frank Broadenax

NOVEMBER 10

Not sticking around

Henry Collins was serving a 99-year sentence in the penitentiary, but escaped. He was able to enter into Tower No. 3 and let himself down to safety and freedom with a rope.

Source: *Moundsville Weekly Echo*, Nov. 10, 1922

Tower No. 3

NOVEMBER 11

Angry editorial

An opinion written to the *Wheeling Intelligencer* newspaper expressed rage as the writer pointed out that the Democrat administration of the penitentiary had spent $300 on furniture for Warden Samuel A. Hawk, but the Republican administration had spent $500 during its time in office.
Source: *Wheeling Intelligencer*, Nov. 11, 1898

The Intelligencer.

Wheeling News-Register

NOVEMBER 12

The first conviction

Spencer Belcher was convicted of "pistol toting" and sentenced to serve one year in the penitentiary. He was the first man to serve time in the penitentiary for this offense.
Source: *Moundsville Weekly Echo*, Nov. 12, 1909

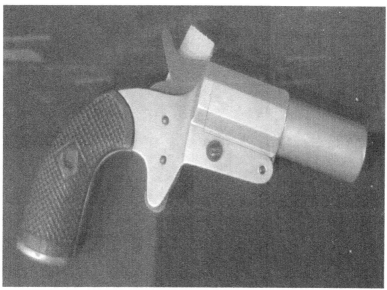

Flare gun in West Virginia Penitentiary Museum

NOVEMBER 13

Blaming a correctional officer

Inmate John Hopkins escaped from the penitentiary by scaling a wall, but when he was recaptured he claimed he paid a correctional officer $200 to aid him in the escape. The authorities did not believe his accusations.

Source: *Moundsville Weekly Echo*, Nov. 13, 1925

West Virginia Penitentiary wall

NOVEMBER 14

Roosevelt Darnell executed in 1930

Roosevelt Darnell and William Holbrook sold bootlegged whiskey together, but had a heated argument over business practices. Darnell shot at Holbrook twice with a shotgun, but missed. Two days later, Darnell shot Holbrook through a window killing him. Darnell was hanged and pronounced dead at 9:07 p.m.
Source: *"Pronounced Dead"* by C.J. Plogger

ROOSEVELT DARNELL   #19630

Roosevelt Darnell

NOVEMBER 15

Escape was hard work

Two inmates, William White and J.E. Walton, escaped from the prison hospital and scaled the walls to freedom. White was serving a life sentence for murder and his body was filled with bullets fired at him during his arrest. Walton was a federal prisoner serving 10 years. The two inmates broke into the tailor shop before climbing the walls and exchanged their prison clothes for civilian ones.
Source: *Moundsville Weekly Echo*, Nov. 15, 1901

Prison Hospital

NOVEMBER 16

Aryan Brotherhood leader murdered

William "Red" Snyder was a convicted murderer and led the Aryan Brotherhood gang in the penitentiary. He had murdered his father and the father of his sister's boyfriend prior to his arrival at the penitentiary. On this date in 1992, Russell Lassiter murdered Snyder in his cell.
Source: *West Virginia Penitentiary Death Book*

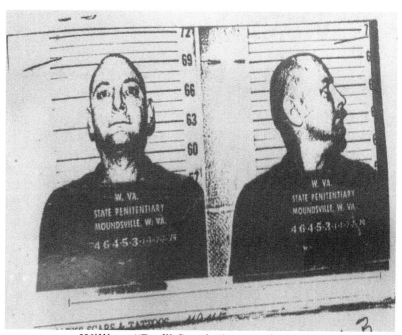

William "Red" Snyder's mugshot

NOVEMBER 17

Not nice to the neighbors

Inmates James Miller and Clarence Tomlinson broke into seven homes and rummaged through them looking for weapons, food, and money after they escaped from the penitentiary.
Source: *Moundsville Daily Echo*, Nov. 17, 1944

Houses across the street from the penitentiary

NOVEMBER 18

Almost committed suicide

Inmate Van Baker was serving a life sentence in the penitentiary and tried to commit suicide because three people in his family had died. In the previous month, Baker's son died, then his mother, and then his only living relative, a brother, passed away.
Source: *Moundsville Weekly Echo*, Nov. 18, 1892

Young inmate

John Moilan, 16, murdered Samuel Winesberg at Bogg's Run and was sent to the penitentiary.
Source: *Moundsville Weekly Echo*, Nov. 18, 1892

Highway sign to Bogg's Run

NOVEMBER 19

Couldn't find turkeys

Warden M.Z. White had a hard time finding enough turkeys for the inmates to eat for a Thanksgiving meal because it took 150 of the birds to feed them.
Source: *Moundsville Weekly Echo*, Nov. 19, 1915

Oven in the penitentiary kitchen

NOVEMBER 20

Give me land, lots of land

In 1930, Warden A.C. Scroggins wanted to buy 2,000 to 3,000 more acres for the prison farm.
Source: *Moundsville Daily Echo*, Nov. 20, 1930

Land where the prison farm was located

NOVEMBER 21

A lot of food

The inmates had a Thanksgiving dinner with more than 1,150 pounds of dressed turkey and heard music played all day.
Source: *Moundsville Weekly Echo*, Nov. 21, 1911

Inmates eating in Dining Hall

Tragedy at mine

Two inmates died while working in the prison mine.
Source: *Moundsville Weekly Echo*, Nov. 21, 1924

NOVEMBER 22

Short sentence

Dr. C.M. McCracken was paroled after serving only three-and-a-half years of a 10-year sentence for shooting his young son on Christmas Eve.
Source: *Moundsville Weekly Echo*, Nov. 22, 1912

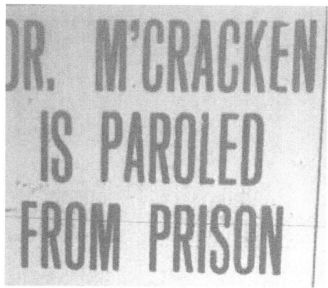

Headline from *Moundsville Weekly Echo*

NOVEMBER 23

Didn't get far

Inmate Ira Daniels was shot in the leg as he tried to escape from a prison road crew in Wetzel County.
Source: *Moundsville Daily Echo*, Nov. 23, 1943

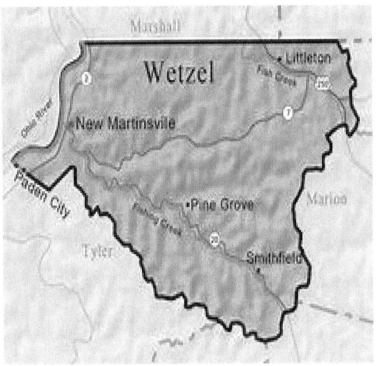

Wetzel County

NOVEMBER 24

Leo Fraser executed in 1933

Leo Fraser, Henry Cano and an inmate's brother, Charles
Harper, tried to stop Deputy Roy Shamblin from taking
Ralph Harper to the penitentiary after Harper had been
convicted of armed robbery. The three would-be rescuers
sidled up to the police car and fired multiple shots.
Shamblin and inmate Ralph Harper were killed. Leo
Fraser later confessed to firing the fatal shots. He was
hanged and pronounced dead at 9:08 p.m.
Source: *"Pronounced Dead"* by C.J. Plogger

Leo Fraser

NOVEMBER 25

Horse thief

Samuel Gorby was convicted of horse stealing and was sentenced to spend two-and-a-half years in the penitentiary.
Source: *Moundsville Weekly Echo*, Nov. 25, 1892

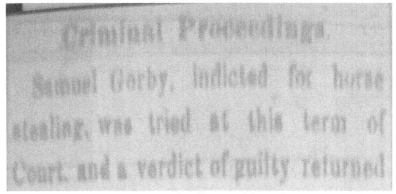

From the *Moundsville Weekly Echo*

NOVEMBER 26

White Gate Cemetery

Prison directors purchased 10 acres outside of Moundsville for $600 to bury inmates after the West Virginia Legislature decreed that inmates could not be buried in town. Previously, the inmates had been buried just outside of the south wall. On this date, they dug up bodies and moved them to White Gate Cemetery.
Source: *Moundsville Weekly Echo*, Nov. 26, 1897

White Gate Cemetery

Bloody day

Danny Lehman, the leader of the Avengers gang, was viciously stabbed in the left eye on the first tier of North Hall. Danny Worley and Michael McMillon tried to defend him, but Worley was stabbed in the hand and McMillon was murdered.
Sources: *Moundsville Daily Echo*, Nov. 26, 1986 and *Wheeling Register*, Nov. 26, 1986

NOVEMBER 27

Working hard

In 1914 the inmates spent hours maintaining and taking care of the Adena Burial Mound located across the street from the prison.
Source: *Moundsville Weekly Echo*, Nov. 27, 1914

Adena sculpture in the penitentiary

Not a good holiday

Inmates Timothy Redman and John Spam were stabbed on Thanksgiving.
Source: *Moundsville Daily Echo*, Nov. 27, 1987

NOVEMBER 28

Generous

The inmates of the penitentiary wanted to help those who served in World War I so they sent $57 to the membership campaign of the Red Cross.
Source: *Moundsville Weekly Echo*, Nov. 28, 1919

NOVEMBER 29

Didn't live long

Danny Lehman, the leader of the Avenger's gang, died in Ohio Valley Medical Center in Wheeling as a result of being stabbed on Thanksgiving Eve, 1986.
Source: *Moundsville Daily Echo*, Nov. 29, 1986

Danny Lehman

NOVEMBER 30

Corrupt warden

Warden John Peck was accused by his assistant C.E. Wilkerson of killing two inmates a month over a two-year period. One of the methods that Peck used to torture the inmates was called a Kicking Jenny.
Source: *Cincinnati Enquirer*, Nov. 30, 1886

Kicking Jenny

DECEMBER 1

Not a traditional Thanksgiving meal

The inmates did not have a traditional meal of turkey for Thanksgiving, but instead ate 250 chickens that had been raised at the prison farm. All of the side dishes of the meal were produced at the prison farm as well, except cranberries.
Source: *Moundsville Weekly Echo*, Dec. 1, 1922

DECEMBER 2

Can't beat a train

Inmate Bill Leek was a notorious murderer and moonshiner who escaped from the penitentiary. Soon after his escape, $500 reward was offered for his capture. While on the run, he was struck by a Norfolk and Western freight train and died.
Source: *Moundsville Weekly Echo*, Dec. 2, 1910

Norfolk and Western freight train

DECEMBER 3

Same choir

Pierce Jeffries was convicted of criminal sexual assault of Mrs. William Vance and sentenced to death. While awaiting his execution, he sang daily with the prison group called "The Hangmen's Quartet" and when it was his time to die, they sang for him. He was hanged two months later.
Source: *"Pronounced Dead"* by C.J. Plogger

PIERCE JEFFRIES   #15898

Pierce Jeffries

DECEMBER 4

Interesting contribution

The early wardens, or superintendents, of the penitentiary did not have long terms because they were appointed by the governors of the state. When a Democrat governor was in office, he appointed his choice and a Republican governor did likewise. In 1908, employees of the penitentiary tried to influence the appointment when they gave $1,350 to the Republican Party during the campaign.

Source: *Moundsville Weekly Echo*, Dec. 4, 1908

Warden's house

DECEMBER 5

Frank Walker executed in 1899

Frank Walker was a hard-drinking coal miner whose excessive alcohol consumption was cut off at a saloon by the owner, Thomas Sanders. Walker was intoxicated and disagreed with Sanders' decision which led to a brawl. Walker then pulled out a handgun and murdered Sanders. Walker was hanged and pronounced dead at 5:51 p.m.
Source: *"Pronounced Dead"* by C.J. Plogger

DECEMBER 6

Paul Tross executed in 1940

Paul Tross savagely beat 23-year-old Mary Stebins and then sexually assaulted her. He adamantly denied his guilt and received three stays of execution. He was hanged and pronounced dead at 9:14 p.m.
Source: *"Pronounced Dead"* by C.J. Plogger

Paul Tross

DECEMBER 7

Correctional officer killed in 1941

Correctional Officer Philip Ketchum was killed in the line of duty while transporting inmates to the penitentiary. He had worked there for only six months and his father, M.E. Ketchum, was the warden at the time of his son's death.
Source: www.odmp.org

Grave marker of Correctional Officer Ketchum

DECEMBER 8

Joe Corey executed in 1933

Joe Corey and his wife, Ada, did not have a good marriage, so he walked into her work place and shot her cousin, Katherine Ghiz, and then turned and murdered his wife after yelling, "Here's your divorce." He received three stays of execution because there was a question about his mental faculties. He was hanged and pronounced dead at 9:12 p.m.
Source: *"Pronounced Dead"* by C.J. Plogger

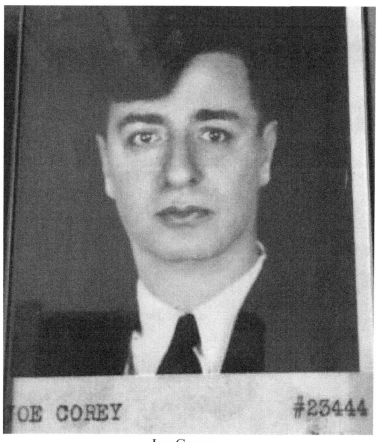

Joe Corey

DECEMBER 9

School's in

Warden M. Van Pelt established a school in the penitentiary and 30 inmates were able to leave work for a period of time to attend classes. Only 1 percent of the inmates could read and only 5 percent could write legibly. The classes included reading, writing, and arithmetic.
Source: *Moundsville Weekly Echo*, Dec. 9, 1892

Education classrooms in the penitentiary

DECEMBER 10

Old inmate dies

Ben Burch was an old riverman who spent a great amount of time on the Ohio River, but then got into some trouble and was sent to the penitentiary. He died during the night and was found in his bed at the age of 72.
Source: *Moundsville Weekly Echo*, Dec. 10, 1907

Ohio River

DECEMBER 11

Not a very loyal wife

Lovie McCormack and his wife were on a boat going to Huntington and were joined by two paroled convicts from the penitentiary. They all started to drink and flirt and Lovie fell asleep. When he woke up he was alone and the former inmates had taken off with his wife.
Source: *Moundsville Weekly Echo*, Dec. 11, 1896

First well

The first well at the penitentiary was dug in 1891.
Source: *Moundsville Weekly Echo*, Dec. 11, 1891

Water fountain in the new Dining Hall

DECEMBER 12

Interesting life

Daniel Shawn had been a drummer in the Civil War and witnessed his father killed on the battlefield. As an adult he killed a man and served 17 years in the penitentiary. It was a tradition for the governor to pardon the oldest inmate every Christmas and, at 76, Daniel was pardoned.

Source: *Moundsville Weekly Echo*, Dec. 12, 1911

Civil War drummer boy

DECEMBER 13

A lot of inmates

In 1895, there were 550 inmates in the penitentiary.
Source: *Moundsville Weekly Echo*, Dec. 13, 1895

West Virginia Penitentiary

DECEMBER 14

Couldn't control his temper

Sam Langford had been paroled from the penitentiary with two years left on his sentence. He did well for a while, even rising to manage a restaurant, but one night, he became angry at a female employee. He threatened to kill her and was sent back to the penitentiary to finish his last two years.

Source: *Moundsville Weekly Echo*, Dec. 14, 1917

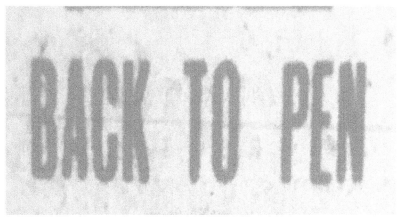

Headline from *Moundsville Weekly Echo*

DECEMBER 15

Prison hospital

A new hospital was built in the penitentiary and used for patients with tuberculosis. It would be one of the finest and best-equipped medical facilities in the Ohio Valley. Source: *Moundsville Weekly Echo*, Dec. 15, 1916

Steps leading to the infirmary

DECEMBER 16

Injured warden

Former Warden M.L. Brown was severely injured when he was hit by a truck as he crossed a street in Moundsville.
Source: *Moundsville Weekly Echo*, Dec. 16, 1915

A street in Moundsville, West Virginia

DECEMBER 17

First telephones

The first telephones were installed in the penitentiary in 1897.
Source: *Moundsville Weekly Echo*, Dec 17, 1897

Phone outlet used for non-contact visiting area

DECEMBER 18

Scary looking

Seven inmates were brought to the penitentiary in 1896 and were described as a "Tough looking set of customers."
Source: *Moundsville Weekly Echo*, Dec. 18, 1896

Too cold

The inmates were working on the large Adena mound, but had to stop because it was too cold.
Source: *Moundsville Weekly Echo*, Dec. 18, 1914

Adena Burial Mound

DECEMBER 19

Chapel dedication

The new chapel at the penitentiary was dedicated and 500 visitors and 961 inmates attended the service. Gov. Albert White also was present.

Source: *Moundsville Weekly Echo*, Dec. 19, 1902

Moundsville Weekly Echo

DECEMBER 20

Sudden death

Inmate Rollin Pelley, 60, died suddenly at the prison barn located on Fourth Street in Moundsville.
Source: *Moundsville Daily Echo*, Dec. 20, 1944

Pasture by prison barn on Fourth Street

DECEMBER 21

They enjoyed it

The inmates enjoyed a "sumptuous repast" of a
Christmas dinner with turkey, candy, and nuts.
Source: *Moundsville Weekly Echo*, Dec. 21, 1910

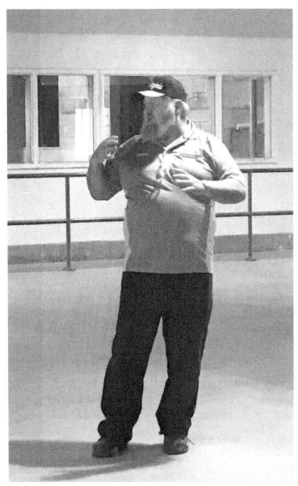

Correctional Officer Chuck Ghent who worked in the
Dining Hall

DECEMBER 22

The penitentiary doing well financially

The penitentiary was self-sufficient and had a budget surplus, so it donated $100,000 to the state.
Source: *Moundsville Weekly Echo*, Dec. 22, 1916

.30-caliber Browning machine gun used at prison stone quarry

DECEMBER 23

Thomas Wayne executed in 1910

Thomas Wayne brutally attacked John and Lottie Ailiff as they were returning home from church and he left John for dead by a creek. Wayne then sexually assaulted Lottie and murdered her. John, who was not dead, crawled to safety and alerted authorities. Wayne was hanged and pronounced dead at 5:13 p.m.
Source: *"Pronounced Dead"* by C.J. Plogger

Thomas Wayne

DECEMBER 24

Man marries woman who put him in the penitentiary

Joseph May served a year in the penitentiary because he violated the Mann Act, a federal law that made it a felony to transport a female minor across state lines for prostitution or immoral purposes. Congressman James Mann of Illinois wrote the act. May and young Margaret Taylor were intimate and traveled from Wheeling to Pennsylvania. They later got into a heated argument. Miss Taylor turned May in to the authorities and he was arrested and served time. The day he was released, they married. May was 42 and Taylor was 22.
Source: *Moundsville Weekly Echo*, Dec. 24, 1915

U.S. Rep. James Mann

DECEMBER 25

Christmas service

A Christmas service was held for the inmates directed by Mrs. Scott and there were Biblical readings and much music. The inmates enjoyed it and Warden Brown said that he had never been in a place with so much musical and literary talent.
Source: *Moundsville Weekly Echo*, Dec. 25, 1912

West Virginia Penitentiary

Merry Christmas!

DECEMBER 26

Christmas tradition

For many years during the Christmas season, wardens pardoned the oldest prison inmate. In 1919, it was J. Wesley Beatty who had served 18 years and was 69. Source: *Moundsville Weekly Echo*, Dec. 26, 1919

William "Holly" Griffith mugshots
He spent 55 years at the penitentiary

DECEMBER 27

Christmas festivities marred

The Christmas spirit was crushed when Thomas Davis stabbed Henry Martin to death at 6:45 p.m. Davis was in the penitentiary for felonious assault and only had a year to serve, but the stress of the prison overwhelmed him and he killed Martin.
Source: *Moundsville Weekly Echo*, Dec. 27, 1917

Headline from *Moundsville Weekly Echo*

DECEMBER 28

William Turner executed in 1945

William Turner was 27 but had an illicit relationship with a 15-year-old schoolgirl. The girl's friend, Darla Pratt, found out about the relationship and was going to report them. Turner was incensed and murdered Darla in front of her father's store in Newburg. He was hanged and pronounced dead at 9:13 p.m.
Source: *"Pronounced Dead"* by C.J. Plogger

William Turner

DECEMBER 29

Generous inmates

Emma Scott played the chapel organ for the inmates for many years. When she retired, the inmates took up a collection of $60 as a gift.
Source: *Moundsville Weekly Echo*, Dec. 29, 1911

South Yard Chapel

DECEMBER 30

Serious need

With 56 new prisoners received in the penitentiary, there was a serious need for more cells.
Source: *Moundsville Weekly Echo*, Dec. 30, 1892

L Block of New Wall

DECEMBER 31

Escapee found

Inmate Alexander Childs was serving a 20-year sentence at the penitentiary for burglary and earlier convictions, but escaped in 1912. He was found three years later locked up in the Kansas Penitentiary.
Source: *Moundsville Weekly Echo*, Dec. 31, 1915

Kansas Penitentiary

ABOUT THE AUTHOR

C.J. Plogger has pastored for twenty-nine years and holds two postgraduate degrees, a Master of Divinity from the Anderson School of Theology and a Doctor of Ministry degree from the Bethel Theological Seminary. He has written a six-month discipleship book entitled One Step Closer and has had several books about the West Virginia Penitentiary published.

C.J. has led or been involved with twenty-three international mission trips and has preached at camp meetings, revivals, leadership trainings, and multiple civic organizations. He is a licensed church consultant and has taught many congregations about growth, conflict resolution, and leadership skills.

C.J. believes that we should never let the love of history be history.

C.J. Plogger

Made in the USA
Monee, IL
05 May 2021